GROW
FROM
WITHIN

MASTERING CORPORATE
ENTREPRENEURSHIP
AND INNOVATION

ROBERT C. WOLCOTT
MICHAEL J. LIPPITZ

New York   Chicago   San Francisco
Lisbon   London   Madrid   Mexico City   Milan
New Delhi   San Juan   Seoul   Singapore
Sydney   Toronto

1 2 3 4 5 6 7 8 9 0   DOC/DOC   0 4 3 2 1 0 9

MHID   0-07-159832-4
ISBN 978-0-07-159832-3

McGraw-Hill books are available at special quantity discounts to use as premiums and sales promotions, or for use in corporate training programs. To contact a representative please e-mail us at bulksales@mcgraw-hill.com.

This book is printed on acid-free paper.

CONTENTS

PROLOGUE: ORIGINS OF THIS BOOK

Grow from Within grew from demand from corporate executives. Coauthor Robert C. Wolcott is the founder and executive director of the Kellogg Innovation Network (KIN), a unique invitation-only forum at the Kellogg School of Management. KIN members—executives and innovation leaders at companies in a variety of industries—meet on an ongoing basis to discuss business growth and innovation challenges and to share solutions. Kellogg faculty members act as facilitators and pursue research in collaboration with KIN members and their companies.

In 2003, our executive colleagues expressed strong interest in understanding how established companies can most effectively build new businesses. Like most business leaders, they were keenly aware of the requirement that they drive meaningful growth beyond modest improvements within their core businesses. They were also well aware that within large, complex organizations, building truly new opportunities outside core businesses can be challenging. It can even feel futile at times.

Three KIN member companies—Motorola, PepsiCo, and Cargill—funded a research project at Kellogg to benchmark current corporate entrepreneurship practices across a range of industries and define the options available to companies that were interested in growing through internal entrepreneurship, or *corporate entrepreneurship*. The authors of this book were the principal investigators on this study.

We began by conducting a review of academic and trade publications. The academic literature predominantly examined related but distinct issues of corporate innovation and ordinary entrepreneurship. Among those that focused on corporate entrepreneurship, the findings were generally too abstract or conceptual to be useful for managers who were seeking insight into how their company should make corporate entrepreneurship actionable. Books and articles in the trade literature tended to focus on practices for inspiring creativity, empowering project champions, managing innovation projects, achieving breakthrough or radical innovations, and creating corporate entrepreneurship teams or groups. The recommendations were often sound and thought-provoking, but it was rarely clear which of the multitude of practices were worth implementing in a corporation's particular situation, or even where to begin. It was also unclear how different practices might support various kinds of strategic, corporatewide initiatives.

Our field research began with interviews with managers regarding corporate entrepreneurship strategies, structures, funding methods, project management processes, incentives, and results. We quickly discovered that leading companies were already employing many of the ideas and project management practices that were described in the trade literature. Companies that were approaching corporate entrepreneurship in a deliberate fashion had implemented systems for soliciting, collecting, and evaluating ideas. Special management systems, distinct from ordinary new product development processes, existed for moving promising projects forward. In many cases, top management oversight and steering organizations had been formed. Implementation of the basics of corporate entrepreneurship management at the individual and project level was surprisingly uniform across companies and industries. We observed no companies, for instance, for which a lack of good ideas was an issue.

We noted three particular gaps, however. First, companies lacked the tools for designing new businesses. Second, there was a certain lack of conviction, even among companies that were pursuing corporate entrepreneurship successfully, about how the pieces ought to fit together at the organizational level. Third, nearly all of the new business growth leaders with whom we engaged expressed the challenge of taking successfully validated and developed new businesses and transitioning them to their companies' business units to achieve meaningful growth for the company. This book addresses these gaps. We hope our readers will find it of value in meeting their corporate and career objectives.

ACKNOWLEDGMENTS

Support for our research has come from many sources. Research funding came from Toby Redshaw of Aviva, p.l.c. (with Motorola at the time), Albert Manzone of Kraft Foods, Inc. (with PepsiCo at the time), David Patchen of Cargill, and Mark Karasek and Dave Rolls of Chamberlain Group. Professor Mohanbir Sawhney and Dean Dipak Jain provided resources, intellectual contributions, and a home for our work at the Center for Research in Technology and Innovation (CRTI) at the Kellogg School of Management, Northwestern University. Jeff Jansma and Fabienne Munch of Herman Miller, Inc., provided their insights, experiences, and an exceptional environment at Herman Miller's Design Yard in Holland, Michigan, where the original book outline took shape.

Thank you to everyone who engaged with us on our research through interviews, references, data, and real-world critique, including (alphabetically) Rick Agee, Charlotte Allen, Glenn Armstrong, Iñigo Arroniz, Dave Behringer, Richard Black, Mike Booen, Michael Clem, Mike Collins, Sheryl Conley, Robert A. Cooper, Phiroz Darukhanavala, Dan Edgar, Aaron Gellman, Mike Giersch, Andrea Hunt, Guido Jouret, Phil Kotler, Nelson Levy, Marty Lundeen, George Mavko, Jim O'Conner, Tony Paoni, Norbert Riedel, John Scott, Paroo

Uppal, Dan Verakis, Michelle Vidano, Joe Wheeler, Bill White, and Richard Wood. Special thanks to Geoffrey Nudd and Henry Pak, who spent months researching corporate entrepreneurship as part of our early study team.

Many of these growth leaders have also been active members of our Kellogg Innovation Network (KIN) at the Kellogg School, a group without which our work would be much more pale and abstract. In this context, we would like to express particular gratitude to Betsy Holden, Blythe McGarvie, and Peter Bryant for deep engagement in the development of the KIN and our research reported herein. Thanks to Professor Steven Rogers for offering the opportunity to build a class at Kellogg around corporate innovation and new ventures as part of the Entrepreneurship and Innovation program. Our work has benefited substantially from the interaction with our entrepreneurship colleagues within the Levy Institute for Entrepreneurial Practice, particularly our colleagues Barry Merkin and Scott Whitaker. Many thanks to all of the Kellogg MBA and EMBA students in Evanston, Hong Kong, Miami, and Tokyo with whom we've worked over the years. Your high standards and commitment make the effort worthwhile. Thanks as well to Rahi Gurung and Kristen DaRosa for keeping us on track at Kellogg. We are forever grateful to be part of such a vibrant community of learning.

Our business partners, Allan Platt and Scott Bowman, as well as the entire Clareo Partners LLC team, provided support in numerous ways, particularly the tireless efforts of Ari Garber and Heidi Johansson.

Many thanks to the people who offered comments and recommendations on early drafts, particularly Debra Davis, Kurt Estes, Frieda Landau, Daniel Press, Noah Richmond, Nathan Wagner, Susan Wagner, and Stephanie Wolcott.

Our literary agent, Reid Boates, is the consummate professional, and our editors at McGraw-Hill, Mary Glenn and Brian

Foster, helped us create a much higher quality book. Author and friend Liz Ridley guided us through the search for an agent and publisher and provided her expert insights into the process from start to finish. Alden Hayashi, senior editor at the *MIT Sloan Management Review*, might just be the best editor at a business journal. Thanks for his help in making our 2006 and 2007 articles a success.

Dr. Wolcott would like to specially thank his wife, Ada, who makes so much possible; his mother, Marilyn Wolcott, for whom his gratitude is boundless; and his father, Bob Wolcott, for instilling in him a love for entrepreneurship and innovation and inspiring him to pursue what has become his calling. Thanks to executive, professor, and National Medal of Technology recipient Donald N. Frey, his doctoral advisor and mentor in the art and science of innovation management and leadership at large, complex firms.

Dr. Lippitz would like to specially thank his parents, Charles and Rhita Lippitz; his wife, Susan; and his children, Robin, Anna, and Marc, for their steadfast love and encouragement. His doctoral advisor, former U.S. Secretary of Defense William J. Perry, provided years of wisdom, mentorship, and inspiration at Stanford and the Pentagon. Dr. Richard Van Atta at the Institute for Defense Analyses provided insights and a decade of research work on numerous U.S. government innovation policy challenges.

Our sincerest thanks, again, to everyone who helped make this book possible.

Robert C. Wolcott and Michael J. Lippitz
Evanston, Illinois

CORPORATE ENTREPRENEURSHIP, INNOVATION, AND ORGANIC GROWTH

[The] time has now come to do for . . . innovation what we did for management in general some thirty years ago: to develop the principles, the practice and the discipline.

— PETER DRUCKER, 1985

Let's start with what this book is *not*. This is *not* a book about creativity or "thinking outside the box." Companies typically have more promising, innovative concepts around than they can pursue. Nor is it a book about managing innovation projects. There are many fine books on conceiving, developing, and launching radically new products and services.

This *is* a book about taking creativity and making it real, about turning innovation projects into substantial new paths to growth within established enterprises. Corporate entrepreneurship is the strategy and practice of conceiving, fostering, launching, and managing new *businesses*—not just new products or services— that are distinct from but make significant use of a company's current core assets, market position, or capabilities.

For many, the view of Kurt Estes, a former corporate entrepreneurship leader at Motorola, is apt: "A company that does not innovate to create new growth opportunities will be reduced to a purveyor of commodity products and services on its way to oblivion." In a world of increasingly global markets and fluidity of technical and business talent, where competitive threats come from unexpected directions, more and more businesses are looking for new ways to grow.

Corporate entrepreneurship is a strategic answer to the challenge of organic growth. It is an essential component of a well-balanced, long-term growth portfolio. The best corporate entrepreneurship programs are partners with a company's traditional innovation programs and new business development efforts, such as research and development, corporate venture capital, and acquisitions.

Corporate entrepreneurship is a vehicle for the innovative opportunities that don't fit neatly into your core businesses. Several books have been written recently about disruptive or radical innovations. Breakthrough technologies or products usually require a new business design if they are to reach their potential, but they're not the only opportunities that benefit from a corporate entrepreneurial approach. Sometimes what appears to be an incremental innovation in an established line of business will grow larger and faster if it is approached as a new business rather than just an extension of business as usual. Corporate entrepreneurship requires innovating in dimensions of an established enterprise that too often are insufficiently considered, such as the customer experience, channel strategy, and value capture.

There are numerous examples of companies that have succeeded by taking modest product or process innovations and rethinking their prevailing business models. In 2003, a top Sony executive lamented to us, "The iPod should have been a Sony product!" Indeed, Sony had the heritage, the brand, the technology, the channels—everything. The company effectively redefined the portable music space in 1979 with the Sony Walkman, at a time when people were not accustomed to thinking of a tape player that could not record. It was Apple's

Steve Jobs who recognized that the potential of portable digital music in the Internet age could be unlocked *only* through the creation of a new business, not just a better MP3 player. Apple was late to the digital music game. Its success with the iPod and iTunes had less to do with the design of the product, however elegant, than with the fact that it developed a comprehensive solution to consumers' needs. It transformed the music supply chain to provide a better customer experience. In other words, Apple *designed a new business*.

To be effective at corporate entrepreneurship, most firms need to do more than just create a separate group for coddling and prototyping disruptive or radical innovations. Incubation is not enough. The right solution for your enterprise might not include creating a separate development organization. It may not make strategic sense for your business to focus on breakthroughs. For instance, if your objective is to find new customers and markets for your existing technologies and capabilities, you may wish to establish a group that coaches and supports your business units in discovering and exploiting adjacent markets. If your objective is to discover and retain the entrepreneurial employees who are already working for you but are not realizing their potential, then you may benefit from a program that moves these people into high-growth areas of your existing businesses.

We'll focus frequently on objectives—your objectives—throughout the book, making sure that you know exactly what you're trying to accomplish before you select tools and approaches. In our experience, corporate entrepreneurship initiatives often become overly focused on generating creative ideas. There are plenty of creativity experts who would be delighted to help you jump-start innovative thinking. This can be a breath of fresh air, but it won't amount to much if there are no management structures and processes in place to turn the resulting bunch of ideas into new business designs, then convert them into growing businesses. How many brainstorming sessions have you and your colleagues attended where nothing much happened after everyone returned to the office? If good ideas are consistently ignored or seed funding to investigate them is slow or insufficient, people become conditioned to stop trying.

Even if concepts spend time in incubation, how often do they languish there without being successfully scaled into a meaningful new business? Or how often are they suffocated by existing business units that are protecting their own turf or killed because revenue or profit goals are applied prematurely? We refer to this as the *transition and scaling challenge*, and it's an issue that corporate entrepreneurs and innovators across industries must face. The real question is, what does it take to build new businesses within your organization, not just invent something novel, *and* take them to market?

This book provides frameworks and tools for the early stages of new business design and advice on how to plan and lead an ongoing corporate entrepreneurship program based on strategic objectives and corporate context. Different corporate contexts require different structures and processes. Each company will set different goals for its corporate entrepreneurship initiatives and for its innovation efforts more generally. Building the right approaches starts with clearly understanding your objectives.

This is not just a book for internal venture leaders or budding corporate entrepreneurs. The approaches described for winning at corporate entrepreneurship are often useful in planning and implementing other innovation and growth initiatives. Building truly new businesses within established companies raises many issues that are similar to those raised by enabling innovation more broadly. But new business creation often poses even more complex challenges that affect a range of activities within the parent company, from operating and investment procedures to talent development and corporate mindsets. This book is about overcoming these impediments and building paths to the future.

Of course, investments in the future are typically a difficult sell for businesses that are under pressure to make their numbers today. It can be an even greater challenge when economic times are tough. A few brave and resilient companies manage to take advantage of economic hardship to expand their market share, but most companies hunker down. Andrew Razeghi of the Kellogg School of Management notes that some forms of unmet customer needs are easier to discern during a period when customers are thinking harder about their spending, particularly those that promise to conserve capital. New value propositions can keep your company relevant in people's lives when they are otherwise scaling back. Moreover, in the volatile industry of telecommunications equipment, Cisco Systems's CEO, John Chambers, directs his management to "prepare for the upturn" during hard times. If you wait to build growth paths until times are good, you'll find yourself behind those companies that took a consistent, disciplined approach to long-term growth.

Perhaps most important, a corporate entrepreneurship program can help keep your most creative, passionate employees from walking out the door. A serious corporate entrepreneurship effort does not have to be expensive in order to unleash those with exploratory spirits and keep your best talent focused on helping your enterprise grow from within.

Entrepreneurship and Corporate Entrepreneurship

Which *great* companies were not founded to exploit some fundamental innovation and built through the drive and determination of an entrepreneur or a team of entrepreneurs? Even those rare leading companies that were constructed through other means, such as private equity roll-ups or spin-outs, typically can trace their roots to entrepreneurs who followed their passions. Many of them arose without an exceptional new technology or product, as entrepreneurship is much broader than technology. Starbucks convinced Americans to pay $4 for coffee, yet it didn't actually invent anything. It did create a unique, consistent customer experience that has since influenced American and even world culture. Some companies, like Enterprise Rent-A-Car and FedEx, invented new industry paradigms, while still others, such as Four Seasons, Virgin Atlantic, and Lexus, created new levels of service.

The phenomenon of innovation-led new business development is not unique to the Virgins or FedExs of the world. If a new company enters an established market without some meaningful differentiator, something to distinguish it from its competitors, what chance does it have to succeed? These differentiating factors can be quite diverse, but you'll typically find something that distinguishes the companies that drive significant growth. Companies that persist for decades and even centuries, like DuPont or Nokia, undergo transformative change at times in their history. David Yaun, vice president, Marketing and Communications, at IBM and a founder of the company's Global Innovation Outlook (GIO) program, explained in a 2006 interview with Kevin Werbach, "IBM has transformed itself fundamentally at least three times in its history. . . . In the 1920s, we sold meat scales, cheese slicers. . . . Then we became a punch card company, and then we became the monolithic mainframe manufacturer. . . . Actually, more than half of our population now is in services and consulting."

Consider your own company. What originally made it great? Odds are that it was more than just a product or service innovation, and the original products might not be your company's core today.

Researcher, teacher, and business strategist Henry Mintzberg observed in his classic 1979 book, *The Structuring of Organizations*, that as companies grow, they evolve structures, processes, and cultures that emphasize efficiency in addressing their core markets. Administrative rules are implemented, and intermediate levels of supervision are added. Planning and coordination are standardized. This is necessary if an enterprise is to grow its core efficiently and hence is a good thing, but it typically discourages or even punishes entrepreneurial impulses. This is the paradox of organic growth. Entrepreneurship enables successful companies to thrive in the first place, but growth can eventually inhibit entrepreneurial activity.

Our work over the past decade has aimed to help change this. An increasing number of companies have been proving that new business creation can happen within large, established organizations. In fact, it can thrive. Throughout the history of the corporate form, established companies have built new businesses. What is different today is the magnitude and frequency of new business creation activity. Particularly since the late 1990s, corporations as diverse as DuPont, IBM, Cargill, Siemens, Google, Accenture, and Target have built internal corporate entrepreneurship capabilities that have led to profitable new lines of business.

A U.S. national survey in 2004 by the Panel Study of Entrepreneurial Dynamics found that one in seven entrepreneurs was working with his or her employer on a venture. Industry observers Dean Shepherd and Jerome Katz, in their 2004 book *Corporate Entrepreneurship*, reckoned that at that rate, this would translate into 150,000 corporate entrepreneurship projects annually in the United States. Given this scale, corporate entrepreneurship has begun to evolve from an out-of-the-ordinary, serendipitous, champion-led crusade to a managed, repeatable, team-based process.

By the Numbers

Many large corporations do better at corporate entrepreneurship than most people think. People generally perceive start-up companies as being the primary drivers of new business creation. While this is not a myth, the contrary notion—that large companies are therefore not good at new business creation—is in many ways untrue. This can be a dangerous misperception that limits the vision and activity of corporate leaders and rank-and-file employees who are considering building their careers around entrepreneurship-led growth. Could an independent entrepreneur have developed and launched the Boeing 787 Dreamliner? Nearly impossible. The resources, capabilities, and credibility of an established company enable this and other types of technological and marketplace accomplishment.

This perceptive bias against large corporations' contribution to our economy's new business development success is partly due to a survivorship bias in our sample set: we see only the small companies that succeed. We don't see the thousands of independent entrepreneurial ventures that fail or languish for years on life support—what some venture capitalists refer to as the "walking dead." From the media's perspective, rags-to-riches success stories make good copy. In reality, start-up companies fail most of the time. Large companies often succeed in generating new businesses, but their failures—how the mighty have fallen—are often seen as more compelling news. In some ways, this skew in coverage is sound. The spectacular success of a start-up venture is indeed a newsworthy accomplishment.

Any new, independent company that reaches a milestone like $100 million in revenues is quite remarkable. For a large firm, $100 million from a new business might be considered a commendable but modest accomplishment. For the public, it can be buried in the company's overall performance.

This is the nub of the corporate entrepreneurship problem. If you're with a multibillion-dollar company, it seems that you must always hit home runs in order to matter. Of course, you've got to take a lot of swings and suffer a number of strikeouts to get those home runs, but some companies are notably increasing their batting averages.

IBM's Emerging Business Opportunities (EBO) group reported to Alan Deutschman of *Fast Company* in 2007 that, as of 2005, it had achieved $15 billion of annual new revenues from 22 of 25 EBOs. The group figured out how to find and develop the most promising ideas in markets where the company could differentiate itself. Between 2003 and 2008, Cargill's Emerging Business Accelerator (EBA) evaluated more than 450 opportunities and invested in 13, of which 2 have "graduated" into ongoing businesses, 2 were sold, 4 were discontinued, and 5 remain in the EBA portfolio. EBA businesses have produced hundreds of millions of dollars in new revenues for Cargill.

If the fruits of corporate entrepreneurship and other substantial innovation efforts were measured more carefully, many people would be surprised.[1] In addition to IBM's successes, Apple's iPod, iTunes, and iPhone are clearing nearly $10 billion annually and generating billions in profits. The 2006 return on investment reported by the 1,860 U.S. venture capital and private equity partnerships tracked by the National Venture Capital Association was about $100 billion. IBM and Apple are remarkable companies, but they are not simply anomalies in the realm of corporate entrepreneurship.

The new business development results of large firms today matter even when compared to the universe of independent venture-backed start-ups.

IBM's EBO program is going strong after 10 years, and it has helped IBM enter a range of new markets, from life sciences to digital media. As the IBM case illustrates, though, new business creation as a corporate capability takes time to develop. It may start small—which is why many corporate entrepreneurship efforts are, unfortunately, prematurely terminated—but it can grow into a substantial contributor to corporate growth. It requires strategic commitment and organizational solutions that are uniquely adapted to a company's culture, structure, and context. What works for IBM won't necessarily work for Kraft. You might not need home runs—a series of base hits might suffice.

In this book, you will learn about how several large corporations have made successful corporate entrepreneurship a driver for organic growth. You'll meet David Patchen, head of Cargill's Emerging Business Accelerator, which has launched several "white space" businesses that have added hundreds of millions of dollars to Cargill's bottom line. And Phiroz "Daru" Darukhanavala, BP's chief technology officer for the Digital and Communications Technology Group, whose team has generated more than a billion dollars of quantified business value throughout the corporation since 2001 through innovative applications of information technology. You'll meet Robert A. "Bob" Cooper, former leader of DuPont's Market-Driven Innovation (MDI) initiative. MDI has reinvigorated new business development inside of several DuPont business units and has become a sought-after opportunity for up-and-coming managers. A single DuPont business unit leader credited the support of the MDI program with generating nearly half a billion dollars of new revenues for her business unit.

The System Is the Solution

As these examples suggest, corporate entrepreneurship need no longer be an episodic, product-based phenomenon that occurs primarily in technology companies. It is increasingly being understood as a companywide challenge with implications for how the company interacts with its ecosystem of customers, suppliers, regulators, investors, media, and so on. Designing a new business is largely about defining and implementing new and unfamiliar business models. A 2006 CEO study by IBM Global Business Services ("Expanding the Innovation Horizon") found that companies that spend relatively more on business model innovation tend to outperform their peers. The benefits achieved were cost reduction, strategic flexibility, improved focus, and the ability to exploit new market and product opportunities.

Innovative thinking about business models helps companies discover compelling value propositions and fend off competitive threats from adjacent players. A promising new product or service can end in failure if it does not have an appropriate business design to support it. New channels to market, new sales competencies, different supply chains, or new manufacturing capabilities might be required.

Consider the telecommunications equipment company Tellabs, which introduced the Titan 6500 in 1999. The Titan 6500 was a transitional product for telecommunication companies, bridging their traditional switched and new IP (Internet Protocol)-based network strategies. Tellabs marketed the Titan 6500 to its traditional buyers through its existing sales channel. The effort failed; by 2003 the company had written off the product for a loss. Soon after, Cisco introduced the CSR-1, which was essentially the same product. Cisco went to the same companies to sell it, but it targeted different buyers within the firms. Cisco knew that it needed to identify a new set of decision makers within its customer firms, those who would truly value the new product, and that it needed to approach the market in a new way. This strategy succeeded. Though the Tellabs product preceded the CSR-1 by nearly four years, the CSR-1 succeeded as a result of effective business system design, tailored to the new product and its alternative buyers. Though timing also worked in Cisco's favor, Tellabs could have found the same potential demand had it asked fresh questions about its path to market. Largely because of improper business design, the product failed. (See Chapter 2 for a more complete description of the Tellabs/Cisco story.)

Lost in Transition

As this example illustrates, the failure of large corporations to profit from their new business concepts is not necessarily due to their size. Cisco is an order of magnitude larger than Tellabs. Large corporations are typically viewed as being bureaucratic and slow-moving, which are anathema to entrepreneurial activity. Small start-up firms are unencumbered by the processes, controls, and mindsets prevalent within large corporations. But large firms have numerous advantages over start-ups in bringing offerings to market. Large firms often have experienced management teams. They have the capital necessary to see a new venture through its early stages, while independent entrepreneurs are often starved for resources (although too much capital can also be a problem). Large corporations have market access and credibility when it comes to recruiting partners and early customers. Since new business development for a company should be about creating value— whereas invention is about early discovery and conceptualization—large firms should do well, given their resources and their market experience. But they often do not.

In the 1980s and 1990s, firms in a variety of industries recognized that their standard processes and often their cultures gave short shrift to what became known as the "fuzzy front end" of new concept development. Since then, the early stages of the concept process have been made more systematic and productive by implementing explicit procedures for generating, collecting, and evaluating new business ideas, such as scenario planning, technology scouting, disciplined intellectual property management, stage-gate milestone management, and portfolio risk management tools. Some companies have formed separate groups dedicated to shepherding and "incubating" promising new business concepts. Mohanbir Sawhney and Robert C. Wolcott advised in the *Financial Times* in September 2004, "Creativity is often serendipitous. Innovation *management* should not be."

Despite these sound planning and management efforts, corporate entrepreneurship projects often stall at the back end, that is, at the point of transitioning field-proven new business concepts into self-sustaining business units and scaling them up. The problem is generally a failure to recognize early on the challenges to existing business systems created by a new venture. By implementing some of the proven structures and processes described in this book, established companies can better leverage their strengths and benefit more effectively from innovative concepts.

Ready, Fire, Aim . . . *Not!*

Entrepreneurs, corporate or independent, are often advised to move quickly and learn from the market rather than lose time worrying about possible barriers to success. While managing the cost of failure (rather than the probability of failure) should indeed be a guiding principle for corporate entrepreneurs, this does not mean that corporate entrepreneurship initiatives should not be carefully designed. To be successful, your company will need to define domains for new business development that are closely linked to the overall corporate strategy. For most firms, the answer will not simply be "Innovation should come from anywhere in the company." Think about it. Do you really want your quality control group to be innovative? Sure you do, to some extent, and ideas can come from anywhere, but the primary objective of a quality control team is to ensure that everything works properly and that the products are right every time. To make innovation happen regularly, let alone achieve the new business creation that comes from corporate entrepreneurs, a corporation must be absolutely clear about its objectives.

Also, contrary to popular belief, structures and processes are not the enemies of innovation. Structures and processes are beneficial as long as they are matched to the risk and complexity of the project and the culture and structures of the parent company. Most companies do not need a lot of new ideas. What they need are better ways to select likely winners and bring the most promising concepts to fruition. In some cases, you will want to have a group that is dedicated to testing, nurturing, and harvesting new business concepts. In other cases, you will want to facilitate potential corporate entrepreneurs throughout the company to motivate resources and garner management attention.

As noted earlier, corporate entrepreneurship does not have to be based on the creation of something that's new to the world or even a radical improvement in terms of performance or cost. It does not necessarily have to be based on a "disruptive" or "radical" innovation (terms popularized by Clayton Christensen in *The Innovator's Dilemma*, Richard Leifer et al. in *Radical Innovation*, and Constantinos Markides and Paul Geroski in *Fast Second*). Early in the twentieth century, Joseph Schumpeter, arguably the intellectual father of the economics of innovation and entrepreneurship, in *The Theory of Economic Development*, defined innovation as "new combinations," or, more specifically, new combinations of capabilities and market needs. While new technologies or concepts might be exciting, they will have limited impact unless they address market needs of value; however, doing so doesn't necessarily require radically new technologies or groundbreaking business model concepts. Firms such as Wal-Mart and FedEx have been innovative without actually inventing products, and even Apple's recent successes have been attributable as much to business system design as to product design.

Even in the traditional domain of technology-based product innovation, Andrew Hargadon of the University of California Davis Graduate School of Management instructed in his 2003 *Ivey Business Journal* article, "Retooling R&D," that the essence is "bridging the many different industries and markets that exist, and building the necessary combinations of technologies and people to make potential breakthroughs possible." Ron Adner of INSEAD and David Levinthal of Wharton pointed out in a 2002 *California Management Review* article that "emerging technologies" are often existing technologies that migrate to new application areas, where they evolve in new directions that create value more rapidly than in their original application. Satellite navigation systems, for instance, moved from relatively small markets in military systems to surveying to fleet management to hiking and maritime navigation before creating billions of dollars of revenue in the private automobile market.

The bottom line: the key to successful corporate entrepreneurship is the creation and capture of customer value, not necessarily being first to market with an innovative product or service.[2] This book explores corporate entrepreneurship as a means of creating value across the spectrum of your business.

What Readers Can Expect

Chapter 1 defines the concept of corporate entrepreneurship and provides a feel for how leading companies are pursuing it today. It highlights and addresses common pitfalls for companies that are seeking to build ongoing corporate entrepreneurship capabilities.

Chapter 2 presents the notion of *new business design*, an emerging capability that is central to success at building new businesses. While this is certainly the case for independent entrepreneurs, corporate entrepreneurs face an even greater business design challenge.

Chapter 3 introduces the four models of corporate entrepreneurship, providing several examples of various ways in which companies have implemented them. Companies may implement different models at different levels of the corporation or sometimes within the same organization.

Chapter 4 describes how you can determine which model, or combination of models, is the most appropriate starting place for your company, given your particular growth goals and context. Corporate entrepreneurship should be viewed as a learning process; you should expect to modify your approach as you gain experience and as your business environment changes.

Chapter 5 discusses the distinct leadership and staffing requirements of differing types of corporate entrepreneurial efforts. It highlights the different leadership roles of top executives, corporate entrepreneurship group leaders, and individual new business creation project leaders.

Chapter 6 concludes by looking at broader trends. In particular, it highlights how new business design and development can enable entry into emerging markets.

Welcome to the motivating, frustrating, gratifying, challenging, and potentially profitable world of corporate entrepreneurship. Whether you're an expert or a novice, or you're just trying to discover how to bring innovative concepts to fruition, we hope you find this book of value.

Notes

1. The U.S. government's Advisory Committee on Measuring Innovation in the 21st Century Economy recommended in 2008 that the U.S. Department of Commerce initiate a broad national innovation measurement effort.
2. Constantinos Markides and Paul Geroski, in their 2004 book *Fast Second*, suggest that large firms eschew trying to be first to market, in favor of exploiting emerging markets just at the point when a dominant design is emerging among the numerous early entrants.

CHAPTER 1

UNDERSTANDING CORPORATE ENTREPRENEURSHIP

> *Genius is spread throughout humankind somewhat like in a gold mine. The more you mine, the more metal you extract. The more men you have, the more great ones or ones fitting to become great. The chances of education and circumstances develop them or let them be buried in obscurity.*
>
> —ANNE-ROBERT-JACQUES TURGOT,
> FRENCH PHILOSOPHER, 1727–1781

> *I like to tell people that all of our products and businesses will go through three phases: There's vision, patience and execution.*
>
> —STEVE BALLMER, CEO, MICROSOFT

A Brief History of Corporate Entrepreneurship

The history of corporate entrepreneurship is a tale of evolution from manufacturing-oriented new product development that was focused on technology and dominated by developed countries to value creation in knowledge-oriented, networked companies distributed worldwide. (See Appendix B for a more detailed history.)

With the coming of the Industrial Revolution, wealth and power grew from manufacturing productivity, which increasingly depended on the application of science and technology. Germany introduced the corporate research and development (R&D) laboratory in the late 1800s. By the early twentieth century, thousands of U.S. and European companies had set up centralized R&D labs to drive innovation. During World War II, large companies worked in partnership with government laboratories and universities. On August 6, 1945, 16 hours after the atomic attack on Hiroshima, Japan, President Harry S. Truman made a public statement: "We have now won the battle of the laboratories. . . . What has been done is the greatest achievement of organized science in history."

Vannevar Bush captured the mood of the time in his 1945 report, *Science: The Endless Frontier*. The report promoted what came to be known as the "linear model" of development, the idea that investment in high-quality science would provide a foundation for new technologies that could be turned into a cornucopia of profitable products. But by the 1970s, many companies had discovered that having the best science was insufficient. They needed better ways to create viable opportunities based on what they were learning in their labs, and better ways to realize economic value.

Some companies created separate organizations dedicated to finding and developing opportunities that did not fit, or even conflicted, with the products of existing divisions or that were too long term for business units to pursue. However, protected new business development teams often operated more like enhanced, privileged versions of centralized R&D than like truly alternative corporate innovation groups. Other companies tried to emulate the flexible practices and culture of acknowledged leaders such as 3M, but these attempts often failed, as entrenched incentives and processes thwarted such flexibility.

By the 1980s, the competitive threat from Japanese and other Asian manufacturers led many Western companies to scale back or spin out their central R&D laboratories and to put greater emphasis on mimicking the Japanese rapid, incremental, production-oriented innovation model. Venture capital financing for new business development soared in the 1990s, not infrequently for ventures conceived by stymied employees who were leaving large corporations. Partly in an effort to recapture some of the benefits of their entrepreneurial employees, large corporations began setting up their own venture funds. The Internet boom of the late 1990s further encouraged large, established companies to rethink both threats to their core businesses and new market opportunities. A few began and sustained new approaches to seeking growth from within. Some of the earliest efforts at deliberate new business creation began in 1999 at companies such as DuPont, IBM, and Whirlpool and continued with entrants throughout the 2000s such as Cargill, Cisco, and Motorola.

By the turn of the twenty-first century, R&D partnerships had proliferated, and many of them had globalized to serve rapidly growing markets in countries such as China, India, and Brazil. New forms of international R&D partnerships are emerging today, fostered by the diffusion of information and communication technologies. Meanwhile, the increasing role of services relative to manufacturing in modern economies has helped broaden the focus of corporate entrepreneurship beyond new products and technologies.

What Exactly Is Corporate Entrepreneurship?

In the introduction, we defined corporate entrepreneurship as the process by which teams within an established firm conceive, foster, launch, and manage a new business that is distinct from but leverages the company's current assets, markets, and capabilities. Corporate entrepreneurship overlaps—and should be coordinated with—traditional innovation and growth investments, such as research and development labs, technology incubators, corporate venture capital, mergers and acquisitions, and spin-outs. The remainder of this section clarifies what is meant by the terms *new business* and *within an established firm* and provides examples of what corporate entrepreneurship is and is not.

The "newness" of a business is a matter of degree, defined by the level of differentiation from the company's core businesses along several dimensions. It is not just about new products. For example, suppose Dannon introduced a vitamin-and-mineral-fortified yogurt. If no other company had ever made such a yogurt, it could be construed as being "new to the world." But if Dannon simply threw vitamins and minerals into the mixer and proceeded to market and distribute the resulting yogurt in exactly the same manner as it did all of its other products, leading it to end up on the grocery store shelf next to its other yogurts, it would not constitute a new business. On the other hand, what if making fortified yogurt involved product formulation changes with which Dannon had had no previous experience? What if the motivation to develop this product was to begin selling it through individual vendors in Bangladesh, which represented a new market for Dannon? What if Dannon partnered with a bank specializing in microfinance that would support the vendors in going into the fortified yogurt business, as well as small manufacturers using local ingredients? In this latter case, Dannon is creating a new business.

You might recognize this story. In a 2008 article, Carol Matlack of *BusinessWeek* described the novel partnership that Dannon (known as Groupe Danone in Europe) formed with Grameen Group of Bangladesh, founded by Nobel Peace Prize winner Muhammad Yunus. Not only was the yogurt formulation new (manufacturing cost had to be cut by two-thirds in order to make the required market price point), but the entire go-to-market strategy was novel for Dannon. The company had to create an entirely new business model and channel strategy with its bank partner to address the needs of this desperately poor population. The joint venture expects to break even in 2010.

We have described what we mean by a "new business." Now let's examine "within an established firm." The typical corporate entrepreneurship project combines ideas and resources from a variety of people, both inside and outside the organization. Even in firms that focus on harvesting ideas from internal labs, the essence of R&D is incorporating and building on relevant external knowledge. To be considered corporate entrepreneurship, a firm's participation must, in general, go beyond creating ideas, making investments, or pushing sales. For example, when Cisco buys a company and simply rebrands and sells that company's products, that's growth through acquisition. If, down the road, these new Cisco employees foment new businesses, that's corporate entrepreneurship. Similarly, if Cisco takes an equity stake and board positions in a new company but does nothing else, that's a venture investment. However, if Cisco partners with the company to build out a new Cisco business, that's corporate entrepreneurship.

In summary, corporate entrepreneurship is distinct from but can include

- *New product development*, in that it involves new ways of doing business that are often disruptive to the core business. It involves more dimensions of change than product or technology innovation alone.

- *Spin-outs or joint ventures*, whether simply technologies or complete new business concepts, insofar as spin-outs or joint ventures become separated from the company in which they were developed.
- *Acquisitions*, in that new corporate entrepreneurial ventures are conceived and fostered internally, not brought in whole from the outside and kept separate. However, "fill-in" acquisitions are often part of corporate entrepreneurship programs.

Entrepreneurs: Nature versus Nurture

Entrepreneurs are born, not made. Or are they made, not born? The argument becomes academic when your competitors figure out how to enable corporate entrepreneurs from within. Moreover, while there are similarities between the classic entrepreneur and the *Entrepreneurus corporatus* species, the context and capabilities provided by the established corporate parent, as well as the constraints, are exceptionally different. Leadership, organization structure, management, objectives—they all require modification if new business creation is to work within an established company. This is not to say that corporate entrepreneurs can't learn a lot from independent entrepreneurs. They can. Many of the skills are similar, but many are not in critical ways.

If you've ever been an independent entrepreneur, you know the intense feeling of responsibility you have toward your team, your partners, your investors, and your employees. While good managers within the larger company context feel this as well, there really is nothing like the feeling of having your *own* resources on the line to ensure that you meet payroll.

When we write of independent entrepreneurs, we refer to *high-growth entrepreneurs*, whom Professor Steven Rogers of the

Kellogg School of Management distinguishes from *lifestyle entrepreneurs*. Lifestyle entrepreneurs found a company in order to build a livelihood, doing most things the same way other firms in the same business do, such as dry cleaners or traditional law firms or accountancies. Their founders are entrepreneurs, to be sure, but they have different priorities and requirements from people who are aspiring to be the next Bill Gates or Richard Branson.

Furthermore, the myth of the lone inventor is alive and well. Despite many articles to the contrary, many managers and researchers implicitly or explicitly believe in the apocryphal Edison-like lone wolf who, through endless tenacity, effort, and genius, mysteriously generates the next big thing. Andrew Hargadon's excellent book, *How Breakthroughs Happen*, confronts this myth: "Entrepreneurs and inventors are no smarter, no more courageous, tenacious, or rebellious than the rest of us. They are simply better connected."

While this might be unfair to some of history's great innovators, the point is that you don't need to be a Richard Branson to build a new business. Many people do it, even some who never intended to become entrepreneurs. New start-up businesses typically increase during recessions as talented, motivated people lose their jobs or become dissatisfied with their existing career prospects.

However, we run the risk of overcompensating. The myth of the maverick entrepreneur may be dangerously misleading, but so, too, is the contrary notion that there is no role for the unique type of person who is capable of and motivated by the challenge of creating new things. Being an entrepreneur, independent or corporate, *is* a unique role, with demands and potential rewards that differ from those of business as usual. While entrepreneurship is a demanding path, it can also be quite rewarding.

Some have asserted that anyone can become entrepreneurial, but it is perhaps true that in such a statement, the concept
of the "entrepreneur" has become diluted to the point of feel-
good wordplay. Living in a society that aspires to equal opportunity and political correctness, we might like to believe that
everyone can be entrepreneurial, that all we require to cultivate an environment in which anyone can create new businesses is enabling organizational structures and intelligent
processes. This is only partially true.

This is the "nature versus nurture" question of corporate
entrepreneurship. To what extent can corporate culture, structures, and processes create a company that is full of corporate
entrepreneurs? To what extent is personnel selection the fundamental issue, in that some people are born entrepreneurs
and most are not? Could large companies truly hire people
with entrepreneurial skills *en masse* and then provide them
with an environment in which they can excel?

Fortunately, the answer to these questions is simple: they're
not the right questions. Hiring or creating thousands of entrepreneurs in your company is probably not the objective. There
is no reason why any given company needs to be made up of
thousands of individual entrepreneurs. One of the authors
received a call from an executive with a large, privately held
German industrial company with the inquiry, "Professor, how
might we help all of our people become entrepreneurial?" To
this, the professor responded, "Are you sure? Are you sure that
you want *all* of your employees to be entrepreneurial? What
about the quality control manager at the end of the manufacturing line? Do you want *him* to be entrepreneurial?" We need
people who are focused on optimization and process efficiency,
honing things that already exist, and extending and defending
the core turf. But we also need people who are building turfs
for the future.

The executive agreed that the idea was to expose as many people as possible to the mindset and tools of the corporate entrepreneur. This would enable those who had a predilection to do new things, while raising awareness companywide as to how others can help make this happen. That quality control specialist might be quite innovative and even become an entrepreneurial leader within the company, or he might not. The point is not that everyone should become entrepreneurial but, rather, that the company should provide an environment that enables and nurtures entrepreneurial activities (i.e., a place where individuals with the aptitude and interest can build new growth paths for the company). We will describe different ways of doing so in Chapter 3.

It might just be that if everyone in your company were to become entrepreneurial, the company would blow up. It might disintegrate into numerous small groups that were pursuing the future, with no one minding the present. The point is balance. Consider Google, which will be explored in Chapter 3 in some detail. While it focuses on recruiting, hiring, and retaining people with proven entrepreneurial skills, and while the culture and structure of the company encourage new concept development and business creation, large swaths of the company focus on keeping the server farms watered and the users cultivated. Not everyone at Google needs to be actively driving new growth.

We are saved by reality. Only a subset of the population appears to be suited and motivated to pursue new business creation as a regular course. While we argue that everyone in a company should at least be aware of the requirements of substantial new business development efforts and the importance of these initiatives to the company, only a subset of these people need to be dedicated to substantially innovative projects or creating new businesses. This can be a morphing subset, with people rotating through it to gain experience with new ventures, then deciding to remain as early-stage experts or to cycle back to the comfort of core businesses.

Businesses cannot afford to cede new business creation to independent entrepreneurs. What if your competitors begin to figure out how to build businesses on a repeated basis? For years, Cisco relied on a broad and deep community of venture-backed entrepreneurs to fill its pipeline of new growth opportunities. The company pursued the "fast second" strategy—articulated in 2005 by Constantinos Markides and Paul Geroski in their book of the same name—more effectively than any other company. Cisco spent relatively little on "R" (of R&D). Most of its innovation budget was focused on development for iterations of established products or for new products to be launched within a 12- to 18-month horizon. Cisco's strategy was to know everything that was going on in the telecommunications ecosystem so that it would be the first buyer there when a start-up began gaining traction. The strategy worked exceptionally well for years, especially during the telecom boom of the late 1990s. Entrepreneurs and venture capitalists alike considered a purchase by Cisco to be a big win, and in the process, the company became the industry's dominant player.

As long as venture capital investments in start-up telecom equipment companies remained strong, so did Cisco's pipeline. When the telecom crash hit in 2001 and 2002, venture investment dried up. Ammar Hanafi, then a vice president of strategy at Cisco, remarked in 2002, "It's like being in the best house on a really bad street." He noted that the company's leadership realized that Cisco needed an internal development capability for emerging technologies. Between 2002 and 2008, it built what became the Emerging Markets Technology Group (EMTG). EMTG leads Cisco's advanced development programs that don't quite fit within established business units. Its efforts complement rather than replace Cisco's well-established fast second strategy. Guido Jouret, Cisco's chief technology officer for emerging technologies, believes that the company's enhanced internal capabilities for new business creation have made it even more adept at understanding and acting on external technology and start-up opportunities. Cisco now has a greater ability to visualize its future, because it is more actively engaged in creating it.

Like Cisco, there are many firms in a wide range of industries that are learning how to build growth opportunities from within. This is why all companies must address this trend. We need to discover how to generate new company creation within our firms. We cannot rely on luck to provide us with enough entrepreneurial savants who are capable of navigating the corporate abyss. We can, however, enhance our people's likelihood of success.

Stories from the Front

Throughout the book, we'll share stories of corporate entrepreneurs in action: managers and executives who have made the case and succeeded in building new businesses and innovation-focused organizations to help their companies lead the marketplace and respond to new opportunities with more alacrity.

On occasion, an established company generates a new business without a formal process or organization being charged with doing so. Linde Corporation, the world's largest industrial and health-care gases firm, created a new business within the company's health-care unit that invented an entirely new product category: pharmaceutical gases. While the unit provided exceptional growth, it became unclear to the parent firm how the new business fit within its portfolio. Linde ultimately spun out the unit for a handsome profit, but in doing so, it sacrificed expansion within the pharmaceutical market.

Because truly new businesses are unlikely to emerge from typical business units, many companies have created programs dedicated to making corporate entrepreneurship happen on a repeated basis. Since its success with pharmaceutical gases, Linde has become more deliberate in its quest for new business–led growth, though its initiatives are still in the formative stages. Other companies have been at it for years and report substantial results.

In 2000, Baxter International founded a team, Non-Traditional Research and Innovation (NTRI), focused on products, markets, and businesses that the company's individual business units would be unlikely to fund but that could expand Baxter's overall growth opportunities. Baxter's CEO at the time, Harry Kraemer, invited Andrea Hunt, the leader of a companywide shared values program that had achieved recognized success, to lead the effort. Over seven years, with support from two successive CEOs and the company's chief science officer, Dr. Norbert Riedel, Hunt's small team generated a portfolio of validated opportunities, as well as a substantial new opportunity for herself. Today, Hunt leads Cellular Therapies, a new business that emerged from NTRI's efforts. Baxter's current CEO, Bob Parkinson, refers to Cellular Therapies as a growth engine for the company's future. The Non-Traditional Research and Innovation team that Hunt built continues under the leadership of Nancy Schmelkin.

Because of its success, the group today enjoys a level of credibility and access companywide that would be the envy of many corporate entrepreneurship teams. This took focus, perseverance, political acumen, and solid business sense, but doing new things still remains a challenge. It is inherently uncomfortable for companies that are built on efficiency and optimizing what they do best. We'll see how the right kinds of objectives, organizations, and initiatives can overcome this bias.

While Hunt's team sought new business opportunities that were unlikely to grow unaided within business units, other companies have created programs to help established businesses achieve breakthroughs, change the way they operate, address reduced differentiation in the market for their products or services ("commoditization"), and just generally beat the competition. Robert A. "Bob" Cooper, then executive director of DuPont's Knowledge Intensive University, developed comprehensive methodologies within the DuPont Corporation to help its established businesses revise the ways in which they compete and find new paths to growth. The program, which came to be known as Market Driven Innovation, started as a directive in 1999 from DuPont's then-new CEO, Charles Holliday, to help DuPont's dozens of businesses fight commoditization. Today, Cooper leads a program at the Kellogg School that brings the methodology to a wide range of companies.

BP's chief technology officer for digital and communication technologies, Phiroz Darukhanavala, responded to yet a different directive. In 1999, BP's CEO, John Browne, challenged Darukhanavala with figuring out how to bring digital and communications technologies into BP to add substantial, quantifiable value. He invited Darukhanavala to propose whatever he felt he needed to accomplish the mission. Darukhanavala requested "a small budget, a small team, and no authority." He was serious. After being questioned by Lord Browne and BP's chief information officer, John Leggate, regarding his modest request, the newly minted CTO responded that his mission was to encourage others to adapt and adopt new technologies, not to develop them from scratch:

We didn't need technologists who would live in labs and invent the future as the spirit moved them. . . . We needed people who could build networks inside and outside the company, understand what our business needs were and bring new technologies to the tasks. . . . We needed people who could act as internal consultants, advocates for change, and partners to our business unit leaders and managers.

By keeping the budget low (approximately $10 million per year in a company with nearly $300 billion in revenues), Darukhanavala forced his team to persuade business partners to invest in designing, validating, and piloting new applications and capabilities.

Pitfalls of Corporate Entrepreneurship

While these examples resulted in quantified success, corporate entrepreneurship can be treacherous. Before discussing management models for achieving organic, new business–led growth, let's consider the unfortunate conditions that can befall corporate entrepreneurship initiatives: becoming too narrow, too broad, or misaligned.

While other factors pose threats, such as adverse economic cycles and top leadership turnover, we have selected these conditions because they are to a large extent under the control of management. Innovation leaders can take specific steps to mitigate or avoid each of them. These challenges befall many new business creation teams, particularly in their early stages of development. The good news is that, unlike the situation a decade ago, many companies today have already gone down this path, so it's not too late to learn from their successes and mistakes. The frameworks and approaches explored in later chapters have been designed to protect against these failures, although they require constant vigilance.

Too Narrow

Given the focus driven by business-as-usual processes, it is easy to become too narrow in vision and action. The ways we see and do things, combined with the significant internal assets that many companies enjoy, can restrict as well as enable our pursuit of new opportunities.

The Efficiency Constraint

There are good reasons why most established companies have a bias against new things. Companies build structures and processes to drive efficiency and avoid unnecessary risk. Intelligent structures and processes are required as companies grow from small, entrepreneur-led entities to large, multidivisional enterprises. Structure, if done correctly, leads to competitive efficiency, which becomes a core objective for companies as they grow. But efficiency can also become a trap.

The better an organization becomes at specific activities and processes, the more difficult it is to change. A focus on efficiency in current operations is fine until the marketplace takes a radical new direction or makes a long, slow turn. These constraints affect everyone operating within an established company, although the challenge for the corporate entrepreneur is much greater. By definition, these leaders are creating new enterprises. Aspects of the business systems they require may or may not integrate with the systems of the existing company. Sometimes they even conflict. Common examples would be channel conflict, where a new business attempts to take the company's products through channels that are seen as competitive to the status quo. Companies with long-established dealer networks, like insurer Allstate or office furniture leader Herman Miller, have confronted this challenge for decades. Their strength is also their constraint.

Cannibalization of existing product sales, real or perceived, can generate conflict as well. Any new business design must account for these factors and objections. Corporate entrepreneurship leaders need to know when to bow to tradition and when to get aggressive, nurturing new channels that might conflict or pursuing new products that could cannibalize existing product lines. In these cases, new business designs will require thoughtful approaches to testing and validating the effectiveness of the new channel relative to the present state in order to build a constituency within the company as well as build a successful venture.

Unlike most independent entrepreneurs, today's corporations must consider the health of the new business not only within the marketplace but within the company itself. Established companies have ways of killing new businesses even after they have achieved proof in the marketplace. General Motors created Saturn as a "New Kind of Car Company." Consumers bought it, but over time, traditional GM policies and procedures, union requirements, and other business-as-usual factors conspired to transform Saturn into "Your Father's Oldsmobile."

Keith Bradsher of the *New York Times* reported in 2005 on GM's foray into China in a copartnership with SAIC Motor and Liuzhou Wuling Automobile, which created one of the bestselling cars on the market: the Wuling Sunshine minivan, which costs $5,000 and boasts 43 miles per gallon in city driving. Philip F. Murtaugh led the effort for GM and is credited with creating that business's success by developing a new business model and an overall innovative environment. In 2005, he resigned soon after senior executives reorganized the program to give greater design, engineering, and manufacturing power to Detroit-based managers. The SAIC-GM-Wuling joint venture continues to thrive, but one wonders whether the increasing encroachment of the dominant GM processes and culture may damage this valuable property.

This bias toward efficiency, with its downside of inflexibility, highlights the need for corporations to create deliberate, focused corporate entrepreneurship capabilities. A critical role of corporate entrepreneurs is to help companies overcome narrow, short-term thinking, so that they remain great companies in the long term.

Internal Bias

Corporate entrepreneurship requires companies to learn. If you're really doing something new, then by definition you'll need to seek knowledge in new places. Many people's inclination is to search internally for assistance and capabilities. This can make good sense, given the breadth and quality of many companies' knowledge bases. It's also safer, as everyone operates under similar confidentiality rules and modi operandi. Unfortunately, if you always look in the same places, you're likely to find the same solutions.

If you're building new businesses, you'll need to seek external knowledge. In fact, external networks are essential. However, finding and engaging outside companies can be tricky, particularly when sensitive intellectual property or trade secrets might be involved, leading to fears of losing competitive advantage. Many companies underestimate the time it takes to find the right partners and negotiate deals, and many fall prey to zero-sum thinking. Existing external networks may be ad hoc and unmanaged, making it difficult to maintain a coherent picture of the company's external ecosystem.

Top corporate entrepreneurs understand that both internal and external network development should be one of their team's competencies. Some companies even change their incentive systems to reward valuable external connections: e.g., the Procter & Gamble (P&G) motto "proudly found elsewhere," a proviso adopted by innovation executives at companies such as BP and SC Johnson. A good working relationship with experienced intellectual property attorneys can also be an asset.

Concept Myopia

Particularly when your objective is creating truly new businesses, you need to retain a broad enough view to cover all aspects of what makes a new venture successful while maintaining focus. Innovation teams often become enamored of limited aspects of their new venture, such as perfecting the product or technology or devising the right marketing strategy. Conversely, new business teams can let their creativity and enthusiasm get the best of them, wandering off in various appealing directions that fail to lead anywhere substantial. The trick is to be both comprehensive *and* focused.

A company's existing ways of operating pose the most powerful barrier to a comprehensive vision of what is possible and even of what might be required. Most managers take many aspects of their company's established ways of operating for granted. You hear comments like, "Everyone knows that's just how people pay for things in our industry," or, "We've always gone to market like that. It's just what works." As a corporate entrepreneur, one of your duties to your company is to constantly question assumptions, not just of new ventures but even regarding the fundamental design of your core businesses. If no one inside your company is doing so, others in the marketplace eventually will. Like top venture capitalists, great corporate entrepreneurs become adroit at constructive questioning of all aspects of businesses, from product and customer value propositions to supply chains, business models, and talent. The next chapter presents an approach to thinking holistically about a new business opportunity, accounting throughout the process for all of the business decisions that must be made to support success. We refer to this concept as *new business design*, and it is one of the most powerful perspectives you can apply to succeeding at corporate entrepreneurship.

Too Broad

While initiatives can become so focused that they become myopic, the opposite can also occur. Gather a few creative, motivated people, and you'll often find that you have more opportunities than could rationally be pursued. People charged with leading innovation initiatives can find themselves pulled in many directions, from building new businesses and helping established business units reinvent themselves to developing radical new products or even transforming their company's culture. The most successful corporate entrepreneurs tend to stay focused on the right objectives without losing the big picture.

Lacking or Losing Focus

A team of creative, motivated people that is pursuing the future is always at risk of having too many promising opportunities to pursue. Independent entrepreneurs often face the same problem, but lack of capital and human resources and the life-or-death nature of getting to positive cash flow can provide a more powerful focusing mechanism. Although corporate entrepreneurs face resource constraints as well, they run an even greater risk of scope creep. As opportunities present themselves, when business unit and functional leaders come calling, it can be difficult to say no. As we explore various approaches to corporate entrepreneurship, we will share a range of solutions to managing focus. However, the condensed version is to

1. Be exceptionally clear about the overall corporate entrepreneurship initiative's objectives.
2. Define appropriate metrics and accountability.
3. Build a portfolio of opportunities that are consistent with your objectives.

The first of these is particularly important. After more than a decade of research into how corporations and government organizations innovate or become stagnant, we've noted a critical point that differentiates many of the corporate entrepreneurship initiatives that succeed from those that fail: mission clarity and focus.

Taking their cue from the military, where every day is about defining mission objectives, determining means, and then acting and evaluating, corporate innovators need to understand the power of *mission*. We don't mean the nebulous proclamations that grace the backs of business cards and corporate lobbies. We mean the kinds of mission that lead to action. Mission clarity means that we must articulate what it is that we are trying to accomplish. Mission focus means that corporate entrepreneurship teams have specific objectives. Many companies combine a wide range of initiatives, objectives, tools, and approaches into a single corporate entrepreneurship team, and by doing so jeopardize the team's likelihood of success. With unclear objectives, new corporate entrepreneurship teams tend to overextend the troops, waging too many simultaneous, uncoordinated battles. Clarity regarding innovation and corporate entrepreneurship objectives is a more nuanced and critical question than most managers realize.

Other researchers have found the same results. Andrew Campbell and his colleagues in the United Kingdom focused on corporate venture capital, a related pursuit to corporate entrepreneurship, and reported in *MIT Sloan Management Review* in 2003 that corporate venture groups whose investments strayed from their strategic objectives were, on average, less successful than those that stayed the course. Lack of clarity regarding objectives leads to venturing initiatives in which "the structure and staffing decisions are out of alignment, and the unit's managers find themselves being pushed in several different directions." The solutions the researchers offered included tying success metrics to value provided to the company's existing businesses, and giving those operating businesses significant authority over the venture unit's decisions. Similar metrics can help focus corporate entrepreneurial groups, but defining and applying metrics depends on the reasons a particular team was created in the first place.

Once you know specifically what you're trying to accomplish, the necessary tools and resources become much clearer. Chapter 4 will delve into the problem of which model is right for you and how to start.

The Culture Change Trap

Building a culture of innovation should be an objective of every company that is seeking growth and relevance in the long term. However, many dedicated corporate entrepreneurship teams end up with the responsibility, either intentionally or by accretion, for building a culture of innovation companywide. This can be a trap. What team, no matter how dynamic, innovative, and assertive, can transform a company's culture on its own? Corporate entrepreneurs and larger innovation teams can have a positive impact on a company's culture, but explicitly acquiring the role of culture change agent should be pursued with caution. Before embarking on this journey, make sure that you truly have the requirement and the mandate to do so—meaning *active* top management engagement—and that you have the necessary resources and access to get the job done.

As Confucius observed, culture emanates from the house of the emperor. Creating culture change companywide typically requires a serious mandate from and direct engagement by the CEO and his or her lieutenants. If the top group fails to model innovative behaviors and make an ongoing, credible case for innovation, real culture change will be a losing game. This is especially true for individual executives or small teams with the word *innovation* or *entrepreneurship* in their titles, no matter how well funded they may be.

One of the worst situations in which to be left is holding the culture change bag with insufficient authority and resources. While limited budgets encourage ingenuity and resourcefulness, as in the BP case cited earlier, there is a point beyond which even the most brilliant operator should not be expected to cope. When the effort does eventually fail, it will be added to a company's graveyard of botched corporate initiatives, shoring up cynical "we've seen this before" attitudes that throttle true, meaningful change. You will have done more harm than good.

Though most corporate entrepreneurship teams do not have to pick up this mantle, many of them do so on their own initiative. They define their objectives more broadly than senior management has requested and set the bar unnecessarily high. Heeding the advice of professors and consultants, some eager teams communicate incessantly across the company, setting even higher expectations and thereby risking even more if projects underperform.

In our view, UPOD (underpromise, overdeliver) is especially important for corporate entrepreneurship or major innovation initiatives. Early on, act aggressively behind the scenes, seeking quick wins and communicating them strategically, being circumspect at times until you've achieved some success. Communicate in depth and often with selected people who can move your initiatives along or set them back. Communicate widely only after you have successes to tout, rather than setting expectations that you may or may not achieve.

Misaligned

The fact is that if corporate entrepreneurs are going in truly new directions, they *do* need to be protected from core business pressures. Separation can lead to isolation. Even new business teams that maintain effective connections with the core can encounter misalignment through no fault of their own as corporate strategies and priorities change. Maintaining alignment must be an ongoing process.

Insulation versus Isolation

Most experts and practitioners agree that teams that are pursuing radical innovation, and certainly new business creation, typically require some form of separation from the company's established business units. Most companies' control and resource allocation processes tend to compromise opportunities that don't fit neatly within the business-as-usual model, and often for good reasons. In general, resources should go to those activities that have the highest likelihood of success.

Unfortunately, this means that new business concepts are by definition at a disadvantage vis-à-vis investments that the company better understands and that are based on proven success. Separate new business creation teams with their own funding and sponsorship from senior executives have an enhanced ability to pursue truly new paths to growth.

But separation must not mean isolation. When a company intends to pursue new paths requiring limited contributions from the core businesses, with no plans to fold the new businesses into the company's established units, a separated ventures group may make the most sense. In businesses that depend on sophisticated technology integration, a development and prototyping organization—that is, a "skunk works"[1]—can be beneficial. Otherwise, corporate entrepreneurship teams that are separated from the core businesses must be especially vigilant against insularity. This is the trap of a well-funded separate innovation organization, where the funds and staffing are available to pursue large-scale projects with limited external interaction. This is a central challenge for the Producer Model of corporate entrepreneurship, which we will address in detail in Chapter 3.

Without consistent, deliberate engagement with important players across the company, the new business creation team will become isolated. An isolated corporate entrepreneurship team will find it difficult, if not impossible, to move a new business out of incubation into an appropriate line of business. Even if the objective is to create brand-new business units, these units will eventually need to compete with other units for resources and attention.

Isolation also enhances the naysayers' case. The corporate entrepreneurship team appears to be a cost center, investing in projects that are of apparently limited value to a company's business units. Detractors argue that the business units would be better at employing those resources themselves. Don't prove them right.

Changes in Strategic Priorities

It is impossible to eliminate the risk that your company will make significant changes in its strategic priorities that will affect the importance of new business creation. Conditions change. New leadership takes new paths. Everyone within a company is susceptible, but new business ventures are at particular risk. They typically have not gained critical mass to protect against reprioritizations. They are particularly vulnerable to economic downturns, when cost cutting takes priority over investment in the future.

Start by ensuring that everything that your corporate entrepreneurship team does supports your company's stated strategic vision in some meaningful way. Ideally, create explicit strategic progress metrics and track them diligently. Metrics make it easier for you to defend your activities while maintaining focus on the things that should matter most to your company. Maintain consistent engagement with senior management to educate them on the corporate entrepreneurship process, manage expectations, and track your company's pulse. An astute new business creation team builds a portfolio of opportunities that enables it to shift its focus as corporate priorities shift. The team members also work hard to ensure that leaders around the company have vested interests in the team's projects. A few fortunate corporate entrepreneurial leaders build a positive reputation and a web of influence that enable them to affect the company's strategic direction, but don't rely on your ability to do so until you've built credibility through tangible success.

Top management change presents both challenges and opportunities. Be prepared to tell your story in a compelling, credible way at any time. In 2008, BP's top leadership changed. In a gratifying turn for your authors, the office of the CTO was able to share with the new leaders the teaching case we had written for use at the Kellogg School regarding the CTO program. Among other data and endorsements from partners around the company, the case helped describe and validate the value and wisdom of the program. Never underestimate the value of telling a powerful story—especially when others tell it for you.

The Pure-Play Challenge

Public companies face a particular challenge in implementing ongoing corporate entrepreneurship efforts: the suspicion (or even the ire) of Wall Street. The investment community has come to frown on diversified conglomerates, believing that the most successful companies in a given industry are the ones that focus exclusively on that industry. Investment analysts also find it easier to evaluate and forecast the performance of companies that are focused on a single industry segment.

While often justified, such stances tend to be overdone to the extent that investors punish public companies that experiment with new markets, with potentially dire consequences for executives. One heavy industrial company with which the authors have worked leveraged a happenstance application of some of its internal technology to address a pressing problem in medical diagnosis. A press release announcing an award for the technology earned the project team's vice president an irritated call from the CEO. He feared that, despite the valuable public relations impact of having made a meaningful social contribution, the company's stock price might be hurt.

Public companies face the typically near-term orientation of demanding stockholders. Public owners want, quite reasonably, to see a near-term return. In some respects, corporate entrepreneurship, like any kind of significant organizational change, is easier to implement in a private atmosphere. There are rare public companies where investors are willing to pay a high multiple for future gains from innovation (e.g., Google). For other large public companies, launching a corporate entrepreneurship effort may require some explaining to the investment community, to show the long-term value to shareholders. (As with defending the effort to the CFO, some early wins help.) For opportunities that appear to be "too far" outside the corporate core, it may make sense to use an external structure, such as a joint venture or spin-off. However, doing so could diminish future opportunities in the space, since the new venture will be more independent. Not only will it not be seen, but it generally won't leverage as much of the corporate core. The essence of corporate entrepreneurship is the creation of new businesses that require substantial and continuous connections to core competencies in order to reach their full potential.

Ultimately, there are no perfect answers to these challenges. The virtue of focus can become the vice of myopia. A wide, comprehensive perspective can lead to diffused, ill-focused action. The point is to find a balance and continually seek alignment with top management's vision for the future without becoming manacled to business as usual. One prescription is to recognize that new business ventures differ fundamentally from core businesses. A popular framework for distinguishing the stages of a corporate entrepreneurship project and assessing a company's overall portfolio of projects is the *Horizons of Growth Model*, articulated in Mehrdad Baghai, Stephen Coley, and David White's 1999 book, *The Alchemy of Growth*. One may think of the stages as follows:

Horizon 1 (H1):   Ongoing business
Horizon 2 (H2):   New products or businesses in a rapid
                   scaling phase
Horizon 3 (H3):   New opportunities, typically premarket

H3 projects, which include most corporate entrepreneurship projects, are likely to incorporate a range of factors that are unfamiliar to the host firm. For example, they can present new sales force requirements; new channels to market; radically new value propositions; immature capabilities for execution, service, and support; and so on. Corporate entrepreneurship management in the H3 context often demands unfamiliar and counterintuitive choices, which is why it is the focus of much of the innovation literature. Applying profitability or revenue growth metrics to H3 businesses makes no sense, as so many factors remain uncertain. Improperly applied profitability, revenue, and even return on investment (ROI) hurdles lead to cancellation of many viable H3 projects.[2] Many of the challenges of corporate entrepreneurial ventures can be traced to the substantial differences between H1, H2, and H3 businesses. Many of the approaches we describe in the following chapters deal with issues created by these distinctions between ventures at various stages of maturity.

Corporate entrepreneurship is not new, but the intentional, intelligently managed version is a relatively recent phenomenon. As is often the case with *terra nova*, there is a great deal of room for innovation and reward. Yet building new businesses is not for the faint of heart. It *is* for companies and executives who aspire to lead the growth industries and markets of the future, or to carry tired traditional businesses toward better horizons. It is for companies that recognize the power of the established enterprises that they've built, and the ways in which their assets and capabilities can lead to growth and profitability in new directions. The most forward-thinking know that if they don't take the lead, someone else will. In competitive, global economies, every company runs the risk of obsolescence. Consistently and intentionally building new businesses and paths to growth provides one powerful, emerging strategy for remaining relevant and prosperous.

As risk and reward are correlated, being a corporate entrepreneur can also be either a way to the top or a trip to corporate Siberia, and which path the entrepreneur is on might not be apparent for a while. Through the stories of a range of experienced corporate business builders, cases from some of the world's leading companies, and a few failed expeditions, we'll help to prepare you and your company for a successful journey. The rest will be up to you.

Summary

The myth of the maverick entrepreneur may be dangerously misleading, but so too is the contrary notion that there is no role within a large corporation for the unique type of person who is motivated by the challenge of creating new things. You need people who are focused on optimization and process efficiency, honing things that already exist, and extending and defending the core turf. But you also need people who are building turfs for the future.

The essence of corporate entrepreneurship is the creation of new businesses that require substantial and continuous connections to core competencies in order to reach their full potential. But beware of becoming so narrowly focused that promising concepts are killed too early, are too broadly ambitious (e.g., try to change the whole corporate culture), or are misaligned with senior management, strategic priorities, or

investors. Common pitfalls of corporate entrepreneurial initiatives include

- *Too narrow:* the efficiency constraint, internal bias, and
  concept myopia
- *Too broad:* lacking or losing focus and the culture change
  trap
- *Misaligned:* insulation versus isolation, changes in strategic
  priorities, and the pure-play challenge

Notes

1. Skunk works has come to be understood as generically
   describing a separate R&D group with dedicated funding that is
   protected from the rest of the company. Lockheed set up the
   original Skunk Works, originally known as Advanced
   Development Projects, to lead the development of advanced
   projects during World War II. It continued quite successfully for
   many years. The Skunk Works got its name from a family of
   skunks that had nested near the facility.
2. Companies that have directly applied the Horizons approach
   range from technology and industrial companies like IBM and
   DuPont to services firms like McKinsey & Company. Many others
   use their own version of Horizons, but the point remains the
   same: match the management to the maturity of the opportunity.
   We direct the reader in particular to IBM's Emerging Business
   Opportunities model, "Emerging Business Opportunities at IBM
   (A)"(2004).

NEW BUSINESS DESIGN

You can't depend on your eyes when your imagination is out of focus.

— MARK TWAIN

I'm not interested in new technologies; I'm interested in building businesses. Often I find the ideas coming out of research are really good technical ideas, but they need lots of work to make into a business.

— BRUCE HARRELD, FORMER IBM
SENIOR VP FOR STRATEGY

Fundamentals of New Business Design

The defining factor that distinguishes a corporate entrepreneur from an independent entrepreneur is being part of an established company. Having an established company behind you provides external credibility, resources (one hopes), technology, expertise, and channels—most of the things any entrepreneur requires. Established companies also generally know how to do what they do quite well, and that's the problem: they know how to do what they already do. They know how to enhance margins, tweak market position, respond to the explicit needs of existing customers, and so on. Incremental changes such as these are distinct from new business design.

If you're building truly new businesses for your company, by definition you'll need to do at least some things differently. This presents the corporate entrepreneur's fundamental challenge: *leveraging what the parent company does well, while encouraging others within and outside the company to make the changes necessary to support the new business*. These could be behavioral changes, new suppliers, different channels, a range of new activities, and even, possibly, new competencies. The key is to be strategic about what you need changed and whom you ask to do the changing. (We're really talking about a political strategy to advocate on behalf of well-considered change to enable new businesses. We will come to that in later chapters.)

The first step in defining what might need to change is to stop thinking in terms of new product or service development and think instead about *new business design*. You don't know what might need to change until you have a notion of how your new business will operate.

As companies venture beyond incremental innovation, more and more aspects of the way the company does business may need to change to enable the new offering. Does a new product require changing the delivery and support systems that the company uses in order to achieve success in the marketplace? Might salespeople need to approach different target customers with different value propositions through different channels? Might the supply chain require enhancement or redirection to support the new opportunity? Perhaps our existing brands don't quite fit the new product. Should we forgo what might otherwise be an excellent opportunity simply because it doesn't fit neatly into our company's existing systems?

Sometimes the answer should be a confident yes. Some opportunities just don't fit, particularly for companies that are seeking projects in which they add value beyond making capital investments. However, numerous opportunities will arise that fit with the firm's business development strategy but appear in conflict with its existing ways of doing business. These situations are often not apparent.

Sometimes what seems to be just a new product will not reach its market potential unless it is treated like a new business. In the introduction, we promised to come back to the story of the noted telecommunications equipment firm Tellabs, which encountered such a situation but failed to recognize the signs until it was too late. Its Titan 6500 IP telecommunications system worked as advertised, and Tellabs stuck with it for more than three years, but the company eventually canceled the program and wrote it off for a loss. Oddly, within months of Titan's cancellation, Tellabs's mammoth competitor, Cisco Systems, Inc., introduced virtually the same product, the CSR-1. Cisco continues to profit from this product even today. What happened?

While there was a lot of interest in IP-based communications at the time of Titan's launch, Tellabs was a bit ahead of the curve in terms of market readiness. Timing was certainly an issue in the product's eventual demise. Many buyers were still unsure if and when IP-based solutions would provide the level of quality required. Nonetheless, Tellabs withdrew its product from the market only months prior to Cisco's successful launch, and Tellabs had clearly shown its willingness to support the product over the previous few years. Timing was by no means everything.

There was another even more fundamental factor. Tellabs took a solid product designed by some excellent engineers and sold it through its existing channels to the same buyers with the same sales approach. The company failed to recognize that this product would require a different approach to the market—in our terms, a different *business system*. Tellabs's salespeople had become adept at selling to their customers' operations groups. Operations teams at telecom operators generally require a return on investment of between 12 and 18 months. Although Titan showed serious benefits after about 24 months and exceptional value beyond that, an operations executive could more easily purchase a traditional circuit-switching product at a fraction of the cost of Tellabs's offering.

Cisco recognized that the strategic planning teams at its customer firms (the same firms targeted by Tellabs) typically have a longer horizon, 24 months or more. With that time frame, the Titan 6500 and the CSR-1 shine. Cisco presented its product to different buyers within the same customer firms with a revised value proposition and ended up with a winner. Cisco designed the right go-to-market strategy to support the new product's success, while Tellabs sent a great new product through its existing business system, leading to failure. Same product, different business system, radically different outcomes.

The Tellabs/Cisco story illustrates the power of new business design. Often, a product or service innovation on its own is not enough to capture a market opportunity. An otherwise great product might even fail as a result of a poorly considered or mistargeted business design. By business design, we include all aspects of launching, growing, and supporting the new offering in the market: the brand and channels we use to go to market, the supply chain operating in support of it, the sales and service teams and their approach, and even the ways we seek payment from customers. Any grossly misaligned aspect of the business system can kill a new product.

Corporate entrepreneurship is fundamentally about innovation viewed holistically, in terms of all the necessary components of a business system. It is about the creation of substantial new value for customers and the firm by creatively changing one or more dimensions of the business system.

Product or service innovation is clearly part of this rubric, but only a part. Innovation in business systems is about creating new *value*, not just new *things*. Innovation is not just about new products, or even about changes to individual business activities, but about how value-added changes might affect and enhance the overall function of businesses as comprehensive systems of interlocking activities.

Every business is a complex system. Established global companies in particular create ever more complex structures and processes with which they build value in the marketplace. These systems not only provide competitive power but also create complex inhibitors to change. Failing to keep this complex set of existing activities in mind when pursuing corporate entrepreneurship initiatives can moderate your success and even lead to failure.

Consider your own company. How often is this kind of holistic business thinking introduced into the early stages of development? At many companies, particularly technology-oriented ones, many of the business-related questions surface later—sometimes much later, and often too late. The time to ask business systems questions is early in the process, as many of these decisions might even affect the design of the product or service.

For instance, one company with which the authors have worked spent two years on a new product concept aimed at a market in which the company had a small presence that it wanted to expand. The company, known for its creativity and design excellence, came up with an elegant solution. At a milestone review, however, a senior executive asked about market size. The working estimate was only $300 million over 10 years, which was not considered a significant enough opportunity to pursue. However, in revisiting the basic market assumptions and targets, the project was redefined to address a $2 billion opportunity. The project retained the same basic product design; what changed was the overall business system.

Similarly, in Chapter 1, we mentioned a heavy industrial company that leveraged its internal technology to address a problem in medical diagnosis, noting the CEO's fear that Wall Street might punish the company for pursuing such a "distraction" from its core business. Another element of that story is a similar failure to consider the business system up front. An analysis that we performed for the company, after hundreds of thousands of dollars had been spent on technology development, showed that markets other than the initial target were more promising. In addition, the decision to license the technology rather than to pursue it through a spin-out or joint venture—a decision that came down from the corporate legal department, based on liability concerns—would greatly limit the upside potential. Had these business system factors been considered up front, the company might have saved a lot of valuable internal development dollars (as well as avoided the CEO's ire).

Fortunately, we are witnessing a growing recognition of the importance of business system innovation. In the introduction, we noted IBM's 2006 global survey of CEOs that found that those companies that spend relatively more on business model innovation achieved higher returns. This means thinking about how you organize your operations, where you engage with customers, and how you earn revenues in an indirect way; combining all of these things into an interoperating system represents the challenge for the corporate entrepreneur.

As Michael Porter's work on corporate strategy indicates, the sustainability of a strategy has much to do with the difficulty competitors have in replicating the range of integrated activities that make up a business. Porter's Five Forces framework, introduced in the early 1980s, recognized that firms and their products exist within a larger system of competitive forces. Competitors often find it difficult to respond to innovations outside an industry's accepted innovation vectors, because each dimension requires a different set of capabilities. No other MP3 player manufacturers were equipped to respond quickly to Apple's iPod. Enterprise Rent-A-Car's entrenched rental car competitors, such as Hertz and Avis, found it difficult to respond to Enterprise's targeting of the replacement rental car segment and its placement of rental car locations in the neighborhoods where people live and work, rather than at airports. In fact, the incumbents took years to respond effectively. By some measures, Enterprise is today the country's largest auto rental company.

The same thinking applies to corporate entrepreneurship. We must expand the existing innovation paradigm to include the full horizon of innovative threats and opportunities. A rich body of work addresses the challenges of technology management and new product development (NPD); however, while these are clearly critical subjects, very few attempts have been made to present a comprehensive, strategic picture of innovation across a company.

Before we examine business systems in more detail, consider the case of one of the world's top convenience retailers.

A Tale of Two Gas Stations

As business researchers, we find that many of the most powerful phenomena don't fit in a laboratory. We thrive on discovering comparative examples of success *and* failure within the same firm on similar projects. This is difficult to do, and it is even more difficult to find executives who are willing and able to discuss what hasn't worked, but when we find them, gems of insight typically surface. Why did one approach work while the other failed? How can we generalize what we learned?

The leaders of privately held East Coast retailer Wawa were willing to share just such a situation. Their experience illustrates the power of comprehensive business system design. Although it is relatively unknown outside of its core markets in Pennsylvania, New Jersey, Delaware, Maryland, and Virginia, Wawa operates a chain of convenience stores with combined revenues of over $4 billion in 2007.

But Wawa is not just a convenience store. Its locations are typically full of coffee buyers in the morning and bustling during lunch breaks and dinnertime. The staff is renowned for going out of its way to ensure customer satisfaction, and many customers refer to their nearest location as "my Wawa." Wawa is not your typical company. In an industry plagued by high employee turnover, Wawa enjoys turnover of less than 10 percent for store-level salaried employees. Employees commit themselves to Wawa's objectives and values, and by the same token they also expect Wawa to commit itself to them. Wawa considers the quality of its food offerings and customer service to be central to its success. It takes the in-store experience quite seriously. Products or services that diminish this experience are typically driven from the shelves like pariahs.

Back in the early 1980s, Wawa made its first foray into offering gasoline at its stores. While this might seem like an obvious market for a company with loads of locations and regular, repeat customers, it was a big step for the nearly century-old retailer. At the time, gasoline retailers with expansive networks and capital were opening convenience stores to bolster their sales and margins, and Wawa felt that it must respond. Furthermore, gasoline retailing offered attractive financials, with the potential for higher per-store revenue as a result of more frequent visits. Adding gas retailing would certainly be consistent with Wawa's mission to "make customers' lives easier."

But things did not go at all as planned. Wawa failed to recognize how different gas retailing was from retailing high-quality prepared foods. More important, Wawa encountered a more fundamental mismatch with its core service-oriented culture. In 1984, Wawa shuttered 34 integrated gasoline–convenience store locations, despite the fact that the venture had enhanced revenues at the pilot locations.

Ten years later, in 1994, then-CEO and fourth-generation owner Richard "Dick" Wood was again seeking significant organic growth and looked anew at gasoline retailing. Fortunately for Wawa, most gasoline retailers had not been very good convenience store retailers. Still, companies have long memories for failure. After a decade, gasoline was still considered anathema to "being Wawa." There were numerous reasons why gas retailing, with its operational complexities, might not be compatible with Wawa's high-touch, superior customer experience.

Wood started by leveraging outside expertise. He had served for some time on the board of QuikTrip, a convenience store chain with a strong presence in the southern United States, and he had a strong relationship with QuikTrip's CEO, Chester Cadieux. QuikTrip had successfully combined superior gasoline retailing with convenience store offerings. Cadieux, in turn, provided Wood with QuikTrip's detailed business plans, financials, and the process details necessary to run an integrated gasoline and convenience offering. Wood appointed Jim Bluebello to lead the program, with a small team in a stand-alone unit. Creating the separate unit contained costs in case of failure and protected the gas team from institutional resistance from the core business. But Bluebello still required support from the rest of Wawa to succeed—the capabilities in convenience retailing, operating processes, and service excellence that had come to distinguish the company. With Wood's blessing, Bluebello assembled a cross-functional "shadow team" of 10 people from across Wawa.

The shadow team had to determine how to build a gasoline offering without detracting from the welcoming Wawa profile that supported its high-quality food offering. To incorporate gasoline retailing, the new stores would require a new layout and more floor space. They would also be much more complex to manage: larger staffs; environmental and regulatory restrictions; and differing economics, pricing, and management requirements between gasoline and food offerings. The profile to the street would emphasize the store rather than the gas pumps. Wawa provided more space per pump for cars and people. The staff consistently evaluated customer flow to ensure that the experience remained true to the Wawa brand. The company was even able to boast industry-leading environmental practices.

This time, the foray into gasoline retailing succeeded. Why? Because Wood and his team understood that adding gasoline retailing was not simply a matter of adding a new product line. *Fundamentally, they were designing a new business.* Introducing gasoline service affected numerous ways in which the company operated, requiring redesigns of the supply chain, management processes, branding, location selection, customer service—really, everything involved in managing and supporting an integrated location.

What can we learn from Wawa's experience? When building organic growth through significant new business creation, consider the entire business system.

Innovation beyond Products and Services

While most academic literature and management thinking about innovation focus on inventing new products and technologies, Starbucks was able to convince Americans to pay $4 for coffee without inventing anything. Well, at least not any technology. Anyone who thinks that the company's creative coffee-based drinks are its primary competitive advantage is missing the point. Starbucks created a consistent, positive customer experience in a range of locations based on a unique brand promise: "the third place," in Chairman Howard Schultz's lingo. Too narrow a focus on technologies or products not only limits a company's view of opportunities but can also create a dangerous myopia. Why didn't Dunkin' Donuts see Starbucks coming and adjust? The answer is that it did, but it failed to recognize Starbucks as a competitor soon enough, despite the fact that Dunkin' Donuts had sold more retail coffee than anyone else in the United States for years. Starbucks was not a threat to donuts, so why should anyone have been concerned? Dunkin' Donuts eventually came around, but much later than if the company had recognized that competition lies in many dimensions beyond core products.

We propose that radical innovation or new business creation be approached as a *new business design* challenge. Companies accomplish business design naturally as a result of involving individuals with a complete vision and adequate authority, as in Wawa's case. However, why should we rely on a few key people when we can extend business systems thinking to an entire organization? As will become clear, we particularly need our innovation leaders to understand and apply deliberate, thoughtful new business design.

A 360-Degree View of Corporate Entrepreneurship

What does *business design* mean, and how can we apply it? Thinking holistically about innovation frees us from myopia, but it also introduces complexity. If corporate entrepreneurship is about creating new value by thinking differently about any aspect of the business system, how many possible dimensions are there? How do these dimensions relate to one another?

For more than five years now, we have examined this question in depth with a selected group of leading companies through an initiative called the Kellogg Innovation Network (KIN). The KIN was founded by professors Robert Wolcott and Mohan Sawhney and is based at the Kellogg School of Management. It is a forum for dialogue, discovery, and sharing of leading innovation practices with a group of member firms. We will describe the process and value of the KIN in greater detail in Chapter 6, on globalization and open innovation.

Based on interviews of managers who are leading innovation efforts at these companies, a comprehensive review of the academic literature, and surveys of a wide range of managers across functions and sectors, we developed, validated, and applied a tool called the Innovation Radar. This tool represents business system innovation along 12 dimensions (see Figure 2-1), relating all of the directions in which a firm can seek innovative opportunities. Much like a compass, the Radar consists of four foundational dimensions that serve as business system anchors: the *customers* a business serves, the *offerings* it creates, the *processes* it employs, and the points of *presence* it uses to take its offerings to market. Within these anchor dimensions, we embed eight other related dimensions of the business system to complete the picture.

Each of these innovation dimensions can help describe the innovative "magnitude" of a company's current business system or the business concepts it has in development: they can be incremental, substantial, or radical in nature. The magnitude of innovation on each of the Radar's 12 vectors refers to the magnitude of the value created, rather than how new or

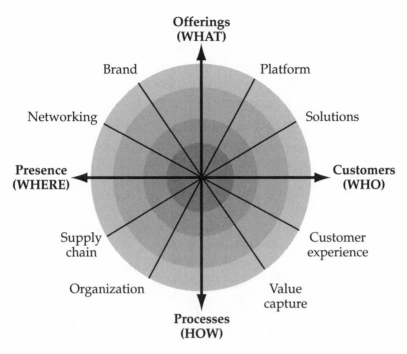

Figure 2-1

different an innovation might be. It is quite possible to have a radically new technology, process, channel, or something else that offers little or no additional value. In some cases, a radical departure from the status quo can actually destroy value. We are not concerned with new for the sake of being new, but with new for the sake of business impact.

We developed the Radar by first collecting all of the activities that companies engage in to add value in the market and then consolidating them into the 12 vectors described here. The Radar relates all of these business activities to one another. For instance, if you hope to provide an exceptional customer experience, you'd better know exactly who your customers are and have great processes in place to serve them. Thus, customer experience is located in the quadrant between customers and processes.

Critical constructs like culture and marketing are not explicitly represented on the Radar. Culture is not a component of a company's business system or activities, but rather underlies everything a business does. While a company's culture exerts a pivotal influence on the company's innovation effectiveness, service and product quality, and so on, it is not in itself an "activity." Management disciplines like marketing, sales, and finance are reflected in multiple Radar dimensions, such as brand and presence, customer experience, and value capture, respectively. Simply, the Innovation Radar presents the range of activities related to providing value to the marketplace.

The 12 Vectors of the Innovation Radar

The Innovation Radar captures 12 key dimensions or "vectors" along which corporate entrepreneurship can be pursued:

1. *Offerings.* Offerings represent a firm's products and services. Offering innovation involves creating new products and services that are valued by customers. This is the common understanding of innovation. Consider P&G's Crest SpinBrush. Introduced in 2001, SpinBrush became the world's bestselling electric toothbrush by 2002. Simple design and the use of disposable AA batteries translated into ease of use, portability, and affordability. No-frills design allowed P&G to price the SpinBrush at around $5, an order of magnitude cheaper than its competitors.
2. *Platform.* A platform is a set of common components, assembly methods, or technologies that serve as building blocks for a portfolio of products or services. Platform innovation involves exploiting the "power of commonality"—using modular designs to create a

diverse set of derivative products faster and more cheaply than if they were stand-alone products. Platform innovation has allowed Nissan to resurrect its fortunes in the automotive industry. (Note: Nissan is suffering along with the other auto manufacturers today. This example refers to how it came back to become the number three world automaker in the last decade.) Nissan was able to use a common set of components to create a line of cars and SUVs with different personalities, performance, and positioning in the eyes of customers. Nissan uses essentially the same small block 3.5-liter V6 engine to power the upscale model of its midsize sedan (Altima), its large sedan (Maxima), its minivan (Quest), its sports coupe (350Z), and its luxury sedans (Infiniti G and M series). Clever modifications of the common engine allow it to produce anywhere between 245 and 300 horsepower, creating enough distinctiveness between the cars while gaining efficiency advantages. While other companies, such as General Motors, have employed this platform approach, Nissan has done a competent job of avoiding homogenization of its offerings, one of the challenges of platform strategies.

3. *Solutions.* A solution is a customized, integrated combination of products, services, and information that comprehensively addresses a customer problem. Solution innovation creates value for customers through the breadth of assortment and the depth of integration of the elements of the solution. Consider John Deere's Agricultural Management Solutions (AMS) business. Combining products and services like mobile computers, a GPS-based tracking system, software, and services, AMS provides farmers with an end-to-end solution to improve the operations of sowing, tilling, and harvesting,

and to help farmers manage the business aspects of farming more effectively.

4. *Customers.* Customers are the individuals or organizations that use or consume the firm's offerings to satisfy their needs. Customer innovation involves discovering new customer segments and/or uncovering unmet or unarticulated needs. Virgin Mobile USA became a successful late entrant in the U.S. cellular services market by focusing on Americans under 30, a previously underserved segment in the industry. Virgin offered a compelling value proposition: simplified pricing, entertainment features, stylish phones, no contractual commitments, and the irreverence of the Virgin brand. Within three years of its 2002 launch, Virgin had attracted more than 4 million subscribers in a highly competitive market.

5. *Customer experience.* Customer experience includes everything that a customer sees and feels while interacting with a company across all points of contact and at all moments across the buying cycle. Customer experience innovation involves rethinking the interface between customers and the firm. Companies like Starbucks, Wawa, and Amazon have focused on customer experience innovation for years. A 2004 *BusinessWeek* article describes how the design firm IDEO helped health-care provider Kaiser Permanente redesign its patients' experience. Kaiser created more comfortable waiting rooms, a lobby with clearer directions for patients, larger examination rooms, and special corridors where medical staff could collaborate. Kaiser understands that patients not only need to be treated but also need to have a better experience as they undergo treatment.

6. *Value capture.* Value capture is the mechanism a company uses to earn its share of the market value it creates. Value capture innovation involves discovering new revenue streams, innovative pricing mechanisms, and new ways to get paid by customers or partners. The automotive information site Edmunds.com has created several innovative ways to garner revenue from its services. It generates advertising revenues from contextual advertising; syndication revenues by licensing its tools and content to partners like the *New York Times* and AOL; referral revenues from insurance, warranty, and financing partners; and analytics revenues by providing OEMs with market intelligence on customer buying behavior. These revenue streams have significantly increased Edmunds's average revenues per visitor.

7. *Processes.* Processes represent the configuration of business activities used to conduct internal operations. Process innovation involves redesigning processes for efficiency, higher quality, or faster cycle time. This might involve redesign or relocation by decoupling a process's front end and back end. Indian information technology services firms like WIPRO and Infosys have created enormous value by perfecting the Global Delivery Model (GDM). The GDM's core principle is to deliver business processes from a remote location as an outsourced service, leveraging the highly educated and relatively low-cost Indian knowledge workers. To enable remote delivery, GDM breaks down each process into its constituent elements using activity mapping. Cross-functional teams in multiple countries are coordinated using well-defined protocols. All activities are documented to ensure successful, timely performance. GDM offers companies flexibility and speed to market,

access to a cost-competitive pool of talent, and the ability to redirect resources to core strategic activities.

8. *Organization.* Organization refers to the way in which a company structures itself, its partnerships, and its employee roles and responsibilities. Organizational innovation involves rethinking the scope of a company's activities to enhance performance, and redefining roles, responsibilities, and incentives. Bharti Tele-Ventures Limited, India's largest private telecom operator, has created an innovated "extended" organization through partnering. The company reached an agreement with Ericsson to manage and maintain its network operations and completely outsourced its customer service centers to providers like IBM, Daksh, and Nortel. These partnerships allow Bharti to function as a mobile virtual network operator (MVNO), with greater agility and minimal asset intensity.

9. *Supply chain.* The supply chain is the sequence of activities and agents that moves goods, services, and information from their source to the delivery of products and services. Supply chain innovation involves streamlining the flow of supply chain information, changing the supply chain structure, or enhancing supplier and channel collaboration. The Spanish apparel retailer Zara has created a very fast and flexible supply chain by making counterintuitive choices in sourcing, design, manufacturing, and logistics. Unlike its competitors, Zara does not fully outsource its production, but retains half of its production in-house to cut sourcing lead times. Zara also owns most of its retail stores, allowing it to maintain direct contact with its customers. And Zara eschews economies of scale by making small lots and launching myriad designs, allowing it to refresh its offerings almost weekly. It ships garments on hangers, a practice that

requires more warehouse space but allows new designs to be displayed more quickly. These choices allow Zara to shorten the design-to-retail cycle to as little as 15 days and to sell most of its merchandise at full price.

10. *Presence.* Points of presence represent the channels and channel partners that a company employs to take its offerings to market. Presence innovation involves creating new points of presence or using existing points of presence in creative ways. In the 1980s, when Titan Watches Limited entered the Indian watch market with a wide range of stylish quartz wristwatches, it was locked out of watch retailing channels that were controlled by its competitor. Titan took a fresh look at the channel, asking: must watches be sold at watch stores? Titan found that its target customers also shopped at jewelry stores, appliance stores, and consumer electronics stores. Titan pioneered the concept of "nontraditional outlets" (NTOs)—an innovative retail format that took the form of freestanding kiosks placed within other retail stores. For service and repair, Titan complemented its NTOs with a nationwide after-sales service network where the watches could be repaired. NTOs' success contributed to Titan's ascendancy as the Indian watch industry leader.

11. *Networking.* Networking involves connecting the company or its products with customers through a network, that is, creating networked versions of products, services, and solutions. Networking innovation entails the enhancement of the intelligence, flexibility, or effectiveness of a firm's offerings. It is increasingly a source of competitive advantage for businesses in all industries, beyond the traditional "back office" venues of information technology. Consider how Mexican industrial giant CEMEX redefined its offerings in the ready-to-pour

concrete business through networking innovation. Traditionally, CEMEX offered a three-hour delivery window for ready-to-pour concrete, with a 48-hour advance ordering requirement. Unfortunately, construction is an unpredictable business. Over 50 percent of CEMEX's customers would cancel orders at the last minute, causing problems for CEMEX and financial penalties for its customers. The company installed GPS systems and computers in its fleet of trucks, a satellite communication system that links each plant, and a global Internet portal to track order status worldwide. This integrated network allowed CEMEX to offer a 20-minute time window for delivering ready-to-pour concrete with 98 percent reliability. CEMEX also benefits from better fleet utilization and lower operating costs.

12. *Brand*. Brands are the symbols, words, or marks with which a company communicates a promise and an image to its customers. Branding innovation leverages or extends the brand in creative ways. Europe-based easyGroup has been a leader in this respect. Founded by serial entrepreneur Stelios Haji-Ioannou, easyGroup owns the "easy" brand, licensing it to a range of "easy" branded businesses. The core promises of the brand are good value and simplicity. The "easy" moniker has been extended to more than a dozen industries, introducing offerings such as easyJet, easyCar, easyInternetCafe, easyMoney, easyCinema, easyHotel, and easyWatch. Stelios sees himself more as the steward of the brand than as the manager of a group of operating companies.

Every aspect of what companies do to add value in the marketplace is represented by the Radar. Every dimension is relevant to any industry, although each dimension acquires a different meaning depending on the industry to which the Radar is applied. For instance, supply chain means something much different to a consultancy from what it means to an automobile company. Although one might not think of supply chains for consultancies, they certainly have them, to supply inputs like talent, frameworks, and methodologies.

While these examples illustrate the many possible dimensions of innovation, the true value of the Innovation Radar arises from its ability to portray business innovation as a *systemic* construct, requiring multiple dimensions of innovation to be considered as part of a business system. Returning to the example of the Apple iPod and iTunes, we've emphasized that they are more than an elegant product and a useful service. Together, they are an elegant solution for both customers (simple, integrated buying and consumption of digital music) and content owners (a secure, pay-per-song model for legal music downloads). In Innovation Radar terms, Apple attacked not only the product, platform, and customer experience vectors—the factors that most analysts discuss—but also the supply chain (content owners), networking (connecting with Windows PCs), value capture (iTunes), and brand (at the time, a non-obvious extension of the Apple identity).

Corporate Entrepreneurship as a Business Design Challenge

Most products and services that businesses offer are merely what emerge from a company's established business system or systems. This makes sense, as large, established companies became large and established by structuring themselves to accomplish specific things very efficiently. The products and services they offer are generally designed to conform to that system. If new ideas conform, they are more likely to be acted upon. If they don't, they are more likely to be passed by, even if they make financial and strategic sense for the company.

We propose that all new products or services should be approached as *new business design* challenges. This needn't be an expensive or time-consuming proposition. In cases where a new product fits neatly into the company's established ways of operating, the business design challenge becomes simple: just design the product and take it to market as you would anything else. But even in such a case, we propose that development teams pose comprehensive business design questions up front, in order to bring to the surface unquestioned assumptions that might no longer be true. In cases such as the Tellabs Titan 6500, new business design rather than just new product development would have made a significant difference.

Part of the problem is that most firms take a narrow view of what it means to innovate. Not only do they leave a lot of opportunities on the table, but their limited vision can compromise the success of otherwise great products. For most companies, their innovation focus areas evolve as a result of history ("This is what we've always innovated on") or by industry or market convention ("This is how everyone innovates"). While we like to think that managers consider and invest in the best opportunities, they often invest in what fits into their existing vision of the world, and what the company can most easily act on.

In November of 2005, two Fortune 200 U.S. food companies approached us to create their Innovation Radar profiles. Neither knew that the other was contacting us. Some 20 to 30 top executives from each company completed the 120-question Radar Survey relative only to their own company. The results are shown in Figure 2-2. Note that the resulting profiles are nearly the same, with only minor variations. Statistically, they are exactly the same. Consider this again: two different management

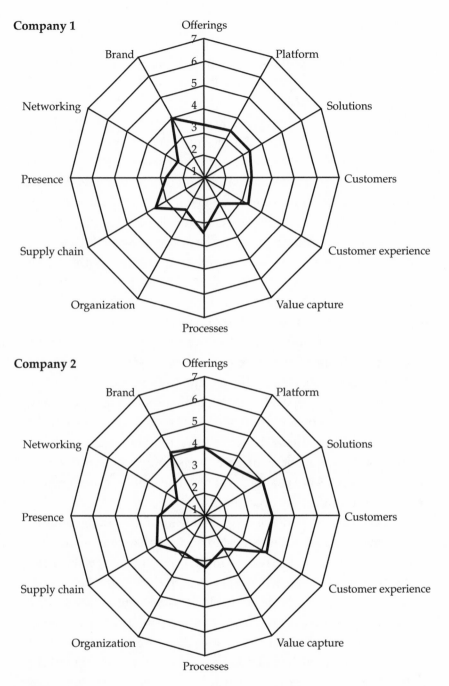

Figure 2-2

teams at two different multibillion-dollar companies in the same industry have exactly the same Innovation Radar profiles.

When presented with the evidence, a senior R&D executive at one of the companies remarked, "I knew this was true. Now I actually *see* it. . . . How depressing." While most companies aren't quite as much in sync with their competitors as in this case, we do see an impressive amount of "me too" innovation, especially when we expand our vision to the business system rather than simply to products or services. Naturally, industries evolve to similarity for a variety of reasons, both good and bad. Companies that end up leading change within their industries are often those that change the basis of competition, not just through products but through a radical reconsideration of accepted aspects of their business system.

Corporate entrepreneurs face particularly tough business design challenges. Developing a new stand-alone product can be much easier than changing a company's supply chain or the way its customers pay. However, if business design were easy, there wouldn't be any money in it. The good news is that the discipline of business design allows new business teams to pose the right questions up front, determine whether business system changes are feasible, test new concepts in advance, and design their offerings accordingly.

More often than not, development teams focus on the product or technology, and business-related decisions like channel strategy and supply chain issues surface much later. Not only can business issues be more expensive to solve as a product nears the market-place—after significant resources have been spent to develop the product—but product decisions that were made early on might severely restrict the business options that are available later. Failing to keep the business issues front and center throughout the development process can be costly, and keeping them there need not be complex. A major pharmaceutical company worked for years to develop a new beta-blocker. At the beginning, the concept looked promising. By the time the technology was ready for market, however, seven other companies had already introduced competing products. By that time, the company's product offered no real differentiation. Failure to track business realities during development led to an awful waste of company resources.

The Innovation Radar won't solve this problem entirely, but it will help you organize all of the business issues up front so that your team can track changes in your assumptions as development projects progress. Early on, corporate entrepreneurship teams should explore all 12 dimensions of their concept's potential business system, not only to uncover innovative opportunities to enhance the business concept but also to define the assumptions underlying each dimension and track progress as their concepts develop.

When your objective is to build a new business, you'll engage in new business design whether you know it or not. You can ignore business decisions until late in the process and default to new product design, but it's best to take a deliberate approach and consider all aspects of how you serve the market: what you're offering, to whom, how you create and support it, and where you connect with the marketplace. The Radar represents all of these dimensions and provides a simple tool for helping corporate entrepreneurs (and independent entrepreneurs, for that matter) put all of the questions on the table up front, rather than stumbling on them later. Appendix A provides a guide with 31 questions to help you think more creatively about how you might innovate around your business system. We'll come back to the application of these questions following the business design case.

**Business Design Case: Kraft Foods, Inc.'s
Tassimo Hot Beverage System**

Kraft's introduction of Tassimo in 2004 reflects one exploration of vectors outside the food industry's traditional purview. The

Tassimo Hot Beverage System—a *platform* innovation—"brings coffee house beverages home," according to Kraft's 2005 press release announcing it. Based on bar codes on the beverage cartridges, "T-DISCS," that are inserted into the brewing machine, Tassimo automates all aspects of the beverage preparation process, from cappuccinos to teas. Kraft has also pursued innovation along the organization vector to support Tassimo, partnering with Italy's Saeco for production and Germany's Braun for distribution and service. Tassimo is an early example of Kraft's aggressive R&D program integrating information technologies such as bar coding, RFID (radio-frequency identification), and Internet-enabled products into the kitchen, thus positioning Kraft as a leader in the evolving home experience.

The Tassimo case also illustrates that business design along each of the vectors of the business system presents the corporate innovator with a make-or-buy decision. Should the company modify its capabilities along a particular vector, or should it partner with some entity that is able to bring that capability to the new business? In some cases, the answer can be obvious, like Kraft's decision to outsource manufacturing, while for other business system options, it might not be so clear. Kraft's relationships with its traditional distribution channels were established and strong; however, it had little presence in locations such as electronics retailers like Best Buy or department stores such as Macy's. The company had the option of building these relationships on its own or relying on partners with established channels for consumer durables.

Unfortunately for Kraft, Tassimo's success was limited by a number of factors, including an insufficient recognition that Tassimo was not just a new product but a comprehensive system that needed to be treated differently from the firm's core products. Although Kraft and its partners, Saeco and Braun, developed a complete solution, the rollout of the complex components was not entirely synchronized. For instance, T-DISCS that were supposed to be available in Best Buy and Whole Foods locations at launch didn't reach the shelves until well after Tassimo units had been delivered to early customers. While Kraft eventually ameliorated these issues, recognizing after the launch the additional complexity of supporting the product in the market, it ended up reporting a $245 million noncash pretax impairment charge to recognize lower utilization of manufacturing capacity.

To the company's credit, Kraft is standing by Tassimo and in 2008 launched a next-generation high-end unit with its German partner Bosch. One wonders, though, whether paying more attention to the components of the business system beyond the product would have enhanced both financial performance and customer satisfaction.

Tassimo illustrates the notion of business design. More than just a new product, Tassimo required new business thinking at Kraft. The company recognized this in its planning and launch, but it learned later how different a truly new concept can be, even if it seems quite compatible with a company's core business. It is often difficult for companies to look at how they typically operate, as this is in some ways what has made them successful. Whether it involves going to new buyers, as in the Tellabs case, or managing the supply chain differently, as we saw from Kraft's experience, business design means keeping all aspects of the business system in view as we bring new opportunities to life.

New Business Design in Action

We propose that new business design be approached as a rational process. We aren't advocating overbearing structure, but simply imposing some discipline during the early stages of concept development. It is in these early stages, before a commitment has been made to invest significant resources, that rigorous business thinking can have the most impact. In many cases, teams address business issues like channel strategy, supply chain, payment systems, and so on late in the process, after much of the product or service has already been determined. By then, it can be too late to take advantage of truly innovative business design concepts.

Like product development, business design should be an iterative process. In the early stages, you should explore many paths without investing significant resources. Avoid eliminating any paths too early, as they might lead to truly exciting vistas. The easyJet's ultra-low-cost model started by asking whether an airline could charge a nearly trivial amount for an airline ticket, say $19. No traditional airline business model could have supported such a fare. After devising aggressive in-air advertising concepts, such as promotions on the back of every seat and video advertisements, the company was able to achieve what at first appeared ridiculous.

Business system design begins with creative thinking, considering all aspects of a complete business system relative to your new business concept. As you collect new information and learn what will and will not work, the business system should emerge. You won't have made all of the business design decisions up front. The point is that you'll have considered most of the right business-related questions early on to optimize your project's outcome. In the outline that follows (Table 2-1), we offer a simple approach to initiating the business design process. We then provide a series of questions that you can use to challenge your team to take a fresh look at any business system.

Our process is intended to be simple. Your team might accomplish the first five steps in a single day, or you might

Table 2-1

Define your target customer segment(s) and value proposition hypotheses.	If you're starting with a specific product or concept, ask yourself who the target customers really are. If you're starting with a vague market idea (e.g., serve retiring baby boomers), become clearer about who you mean (e.g., retiring baby boomers moving south who are not ready for retirement) and their assumed need.
Explore the business system to uncover how various dimensions might be changed/designed to enhance customer value.	At the first pass, just let the ideas flow. Don't worry about feasibility. You'll prioritize and test your ideas after you have the options on the table.
Refine and select your business system concepts to explore in more detail the range of business system ideas.	You might be overwhelmed by how many ideas you can create around one central concept. Prioritization in the first session means a simple "gut check" regarding which ideas appear to have the most potential for value creation and differentiation.
Prioritize the uncertainties related to each innovative concept.	New ideas present various types of uncertainties, in the general categories of product (can we make it?), market (will our target customer buy it?), financial (how will development be funded?), and organizational (can I get the internal support needed?). Uncover and discuss them, emphasizing your priority ideas. Think particularly about potential competitive threats or collaborative opportunities.
Design simple experiments and build your action plan to resolve the uncertainties and refine your knowledge. Create your action plan with learning milestones.	Experiments can be as simple as calling some relevant experts for advice or some basic market research, or as complex as a major system experiment. Your action plan should articulate what knowledge you're hoping to gain.
Iterate until you've settled on the right business system for the market.	Business system design should occur in parallel with product/service development, not as a by-product of it.

extend the process over months. We recommend making a first pass quickly, say, in a day or two. Cycle through the process once, then return after you've learned more and iterate, taking more time the second time around. Innovation is a highly path-dependent process. The more focused on one path you become, the more difficult it will be to shift gears when you get new information. At some point you'll need to have everyone driving in the same direction, but for goodness sake, don't lock in that direction too early. We see this all too often. Someone in the company comes up with a good idea and starts to pursue it, but in doing so, the person focuses on an initial hunch rather than exploring perhaps even better market opportunities. Being too focused early on causes people to ignore or dismiss information that does not fit. Leave plenty of time to iterate and try multiple paths. Your eventual business system design is bound to be more competitive.

For critical new product programs, Toyota Motor Corporation assigns multiple parallel design teams to develop various visions of the product. The company later selects among them and incorporates insights from each into the final product. Clearly this is a more costly process, but keep in mind that development costs in the early design stages are relatively small compared to the resource commitments later in the design process. Toyota finds its ultimate outcomes to be vastly improved, as the competitive process brings more alternatives to the surface and brings forward more disparate knowledge in the early stages, when the project concept is more malleable. The same can be said for new business design. Although most companies do not have the resources to assign parallel teams to the same project, allowing business design teams the opportunity to iterate early on employs similar wisdom.

Step 1: Define Your Target Customer Segment(s) and Value Proposition Hypotheses

Everything in business should start with the customer. New business design is no exception. Unfortunately, the customer is not always as obvious as he or she might seem to be. Pioneers in innovation are recognizing that articulating and validating market needs early might be as important as, or even more important than, finding and developing technologies or products. Development teams are more likely to generate high-quality solutions if they have a clear idea of what needs they are attempting to address. Your innovative concept may be valuable for your existing customers, or it may not be. Although customers can be a rich source of innovative ideas, they are typically not good at thinking beyond what already exists, a limitation of most customer surveys and focus groups. As Clayton M. Christensen showed in his 1997 book *The Innovator's Dilemma*, existing customers may be particularly disposed against truly new concepts, especially if those concepts are disruptive. If you rely only on your existing customers, you're likely to nix many potentially powerful opportunities. New ideas often appeal to entirely new customers, or perhaps new segments of the same customer populations that you already serve. Substantial, game-changing innovation often comes from discovering needs that customers don't even know they have until those needs are fulfilled. Customer insight methods and market research have matured over the past decade, both quantitatively and qualitatively. Examples include empathic design, ethnographic research, and customer activity cycle mapping.

Great ideas have certainly come without the customer in mind. However, if they eventually succeed in the marketplace, it is only because they found the *right* customers, either deliberately or by accident. Start by developing a solid hypothesis to identify your target customers. What is the relevant problem that is being solved? What pain is being alleviated? Place the emphasis on *hypothesis*, as all you really know in the early stages of a truly innovative project is that you don't really know for sure, but you must start somewhere.

So, select and define the customer segment or segments that you believe will become your target(s). Then define the underlying value propositions as best you can from the customers' perspectives. There are many frameworks and experts available to help you discover and define value propositions. We won't describe them all here; however, we will share a simple, powerful framework developed by our colleague at Kellogg, Mohanbir Sawhney. The Sawhney framework, shown in Figure 2-3, illustrates that customer value propositions include both benefits and costs. Most companies focus on the benefits and perhaps the financial costs to customers of acquiring and using a new offering. Unfortunately, adopting a new technology, service, process, or something else introduces costs to the customer. Some of these costs can be negligible, such as substituting one similar product for another. Others can be quite costly from a financial and organizational perspective, such as installing a new suite of enterprisewide software. Such an introduction requires people to change their behavior and work patterns, an often challenging and sometimes wrenching process.

After you have defined the target customer or customers, ask yourself the following questions *from your customer's* perspective.

Benefits

What's in It for Me? What is your offering's *promise* to the customer? Articulating this notion up front will help you think

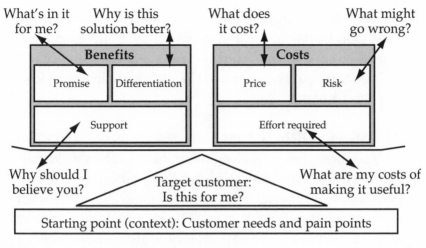

Figure 2-3   Defining Value Propositions

more effectively about what you're building and how to communicate it. Fred Smith's original promise at FedEx was overnight, on time, secure delivery. This presented a range of business model and capabilities design challenges that the company finally met to become the industry leader. Define your promise succinctly, and make sure that it is meaningful to the customer. Hopefully, you'll spend most of your time designing your products, services, and business models to support this promise.

Why Is This Solution Better? Explain what meaningfully *differentiates* your solution from the competition or from alternative solutions. Your competition is not always what you might think. For instance, the immensely successful online customer relationship management (CRM) service provider Salesforce.com recognized its competition as being not only complex, expensive offerings from large CRM providers like Siebel Systems but also the Microsoft Excel spreadsheets, Microsoft Word documents, or other tools that many sales and business development professionals create instead of using CRM tools to manage their sales efforts. Salesforce.com knew that its original target customers, sales teams at smaller and midsized companies, were most likely to be using these low-cost alternatives.

Why Should I Believe You? Promises are meaningful when we trust those who are making the promises. Why should your customers believe what you say? For years, people in the information technology industry used to say, "No one ever got fired for buying IBM." Because IBM had such a strong and resilient reputation in its industry, no one questioned a decision to do business with IBM. The firm's reputation decreases a customer's perceived risk in selecting it as a vendor, thus increasing the strength of its proposed value propositions.

Consider whether your company has a long history of providing related value propositions or working with other customer segments that might validate your assertions. Perhaps you have a trusted brand, but your company is offering something new. Consider whether you have what marketers call "brand permission" to provide this service. You have brand permission if the product or service you are selling is consistent with your company's brand identity and the role that customers see you playing. To use an extreme example, Microsoft might have brand permission to introduce a line of laser printers, but the company probably doesn't have brand permission to launch a chain of luxury boutique hotels. This is not to say that it couldn't do so, just that it probably wouldn't make sense to consumers for Microsoft to play in this arena. Other options exist, such as partnerships with companies with relevant brands, but in a competitive marketplace, it's important to validate why customers will believe you over others.

Costs

What Does It Cost? We're referring to the cost to the customer, or the quantifiable price. Often, teams developing new products or businesses focus on this factor but neglect other components of the overall cost to the customer. In assessing your value proposition, take the customer's perspective. Consider costs like changing the supplier relationship, emotional cost, or career risk.

What Might Go Wrong? While setting the right pricing strategy can be challenging and critical, people too often fail to consider the range of nonmonetary costs to their customers. Take some time to consider what risks your customer might incur by doing business with you. Some critical risks may not be obvious. For example, if your customer's people need to change the way they work to apply your offering, there might be more risk beyond whether your product works or whether your company delivers. Your customers could encounter internal resistance, unnerved employees, and other such results. Think broadly. If you're unsure, call potential customers and ask. It is important that you get this right so that you can account for these costs in your business design. Clarity will help your sales and marketing people after launch.

What Are My Costs of Making It Useful? Never forget your customers' implementation costs. Training? Reorganization? Even issues as apparently simple as changing the way your customer pays you might involve an administrative cost that you might miss if you're not careful. There could also be more involved preparations or complementary technologies, products, or services required if your customers are to garner full value. Consider all potential costs for your customers, and design your business to minimize or at least account for them.

Answer each question in both qualitative and quantitative ways. When you're done, you should have both a quantitative cost/benefit analysis and a set of qualitative costs and benefits from the customer's perspective. You can use this knowledge to

1. Guide the definition and development of your offering, business design, and development plan. Your team can design the business to enhance the benefits and decrease the costs from the customer's perspective, not just add more features.
2. Ensure that your new business supports robust marketing strategy and messages. An up-front focus on customer value aligns the activities of both the development and marketing teams. You'll be more likely to create something that your sales teams can sell.

When you do this well, everyone knows what's being developed and how it's going to be sold. Rigorous definition of value propositions takes more time than most people expect, and certainly more time than most companies spend. Taking this rigorous approach ensures that you're always thinking about customer value while building your new business, which is why new business teams should take the time *up front*. This is not something to work through once you're nearing launch.

Remember that whatever you believe the costs and benefits to be, until you have definitive data to prove it, you've just got hypotheses. Treat them as such. Build your development plan to test these value proposition hypotheses. This could include surveys—asking people what they want—but you don't really know what someone will pay and how much total value people will perceive until they are actually paying you for it. People will say one thing and do something else. Keep this in mind as you build your development plan, and consider piloting in small steps to gather real market data for your new business.

Step 2: Explore the Business System

Once you have an initial picture of your concept's value proposition, start to expand your thinking. You can afford to let your minds wander a bit at this point. It doesn't cost much, because it's all just supposition and creativity. The point is to avoid getting too focused on a limited path too early. You might think that you have the best path to the future and then end up missing a related idea that could have been transformative. Spend the time up front, when it's cheap, generating many possible ideas: channels to market, services, customer experience enhancements, and so on.

The Innovation Radar offers a way to structure your brainstorming. Appendix A provides a guide with 31 questions to help you think more creatively about how you might innovate around your business system. Spend some time perusing the Radar, exploring what innovation along each of the dimensions might mean. Always tie this discussion back to the underlying value proposition for both your customers and your company. Consider what you're selling, to whom, how, and through which channels. Generate as many ideas as you can. Don't worry at this point if some of them seem infeasible or unlikely. It's important that you expand your thinking early. It requires little time and money at the outset. If you have more paths from which to choose early on, you're more likely to take a good one.

Step 3: Refine and Select Your Business System Concepts

Select the business system concepts you plan to examine in detail. Which business model concepts seem to have the most merit? Which could add the most value if you were able to make them happen? After you have selected your priority concepts, see if there are any that are mutually exclusive. In other words, are there any cases where, if you select one, you can't select the other? For instance, if you decide to leverage an existing dealer network, would this preclude you from selling online directly to consumers? Start to build hypothetical business systems that fit together and make sense. As you do so, one or more likely business designs will become clear.

Once you start to visualize a more comprehensive business design—a conceptual prototype, really—note that it is still just hypothetical. The next step will be to build your plan to gather information, run experiments, talk to people, or do whatever it is that you need to do to learn what's necessary to design a complete, effective business system. In this early stage, you still have the luxury of selecting more than one possible business design.

Step 4: Prioritize the Uncertainties

At this point, all you'll have will be assumptions and hypotheses based on them, whether they are about value propositions, production costs, legal factors, internal organizational challenges, or anything else that you don't know *for sure*. Based on your hypothesized business system designs, consider what uncertainties you have. What do you need to know to be confident that you've got the right business design? What do you have a good feeling about, but need solid data to dispute or refute?

This is an obvious step, but too many entrepreneurs, corporate or independent, fail to take a rigorous approach to uncertainties. They assume what they know and know what they assume, so they end up missing critical issues.

While you're building your plan, you'll find that you have to make certain assumptions. Assumptions are simply educated propositions about the way the world is (e.g., "people will love this feature") or about what you should do as a result (e.g., "we should charge $100 for this service"), but they are not based on complete information. If you had complete, solid data, you wouldn't need assumptions. For instance, *you never know for sure whether people will pay a certain price until they pay you.*

Assumptions have a nasty way of becoming facts during the development process, particularly after senior management approves an action plan. When people see that the CEO has signed off on a plan, they tend to start believing the assumptions involved as if they are representative of the way the world is, even though they may still be just educated, well-researched guesses. Remain vigilant in tracking your uncertainties and assumptions to avoid being misled by your own brilliance.

We recommend listing all uncertainties in four categories, as noted in the following list:[1]

1. Product and/or service: Will it work?
2. Market: Will people buy it?
3. Resource: What will we have at risk?
4. Organizational: What internal organizational uncertainties exist?

Companies too often overlook the fourth category, organizational risk. This is perhaps the most important for corporate entrepreneurs. We can do things to test the market, ensure that the product works, or design a brand message that resonates, but we can't always be sure how our colleagues across the company might react. This requires substantial political acumen and networking skills, described in other chapters of this book. Addressing organizational and resource uncertainties is the foundation of the four models of corporate entrepreneurship that we will introduce in Chapter 3.

Prioritize the uncertainties based on

- Importance of resolution
- Cost to resolve

In your development plan, try to resolve the most critical uncertainties early on. If the experiments or activities necessary to resolve high-impact uncertainties are too costly in the beginning, try to break the issue into smaller pieces that can be tested inexpensively. Engineers do this often. Before deploying a new satellite into orbit, they'll rigorously lab test subcomponents. Breaking the uncertainties into smaller, easier-to-test pieces is typically possible. If it's not, then it's okay to postpone some uncertainty testing, but make sure you don't defer for too long any issues that could kill the project. This is the essence of building a smart, risk-mitigating development plan.

Step 5: Design Simple Experiments and Build Your Action Plan

For the early stage, keep it simple. Drive as much uncertainty out of the system with as little resource commitment as possible. If you prioritize your uncertainties properly, you should be able to move things along at little cost to the company, substantially decreasing risk. Risk increases as you spend more money on a project, so try to resolve the simple, high-value uncertainties early on.

Step 6: Iterate

If you're doing things right, this is just the first step. As you experiment, socialize, gather information, and learn about your concept, you'll find that your perspective changes—in fact, that it changes markedly. We were once involved with a company that was seeking applications for a technology that had originally been designed for the shipping industry. It ended up being successfully commercialized in the beef industry, and the business system the company used wasn't a "product" per se, but rather a pay-by-the-use diagnostic system accessed by its clients online. This was truly a new business design, far beyond the original product, use, and market concept. No one on the new business design team was even close to guessing where the path would take them at the outset, but they followed where their investigations took them and recognized the opportunities along the way.

New business design is an iterative process with many interdependencies. Product and service design might affect how you need to go to market, and your go-to-market strategy might affect your product or service design. The way you capture value or the way people pay you might influence how you service and support your customers, and so on. Keeping the dimensions of a complete business system in mind along the way, as well as knowing when to lock some elements down and when to keep them flexible, is one of the most challenging aspects of succeeding at corporate entrepreneurship.

Summary

New business creation should be approached as a *new business design* challenge. There are 12 dimensions that need to be considered and combined into a complete definition of your new business, or at least the range of solutions that might develop into an operational new business:

1. Offerings
2. Platform
3. Solutions

4. Customers
5. Customer experience
6. Value capture
7. Processes
8. Organization
9. Supply chain
10. Presence
11. Networking
12. Brand

Business system design should occur in parallel with product or service development, not as a by-product of it. We recommend that the following steps be included in your business design process:

1. Define your target customer segment(s) and value proposition hypotheses.
2. Explore the business system to determine how various dimensions might be changed or designed to enhance customer value.
3. Refine and select the business system concepts to explore in more detail.
4. Prioritize the uncertainties related to each innovative concept.
5. Design simple experiments and build your action plan to resolve the uncertainties and refine your knowledge. Focus your action plan around milestones based on explicit learning goals.
6. Iterate until you've settled on the right business system for the market.

Note

1. For a useful, thoughtful description of using this four-risk framework to help build project plans, see Rice et al. (2008).

CHAPTER 3

EMERGING MODELS OF CORPORATE ENTREPRENEURSHIP

A corporation is a living organism; it has to continue to shed its skin. Methods have to change. Focus has to change. Values have to change. The sum total of those changes is transformation.

—ANDREW GROVE, FOUNDER AND
FORMER PRESIDENT AND CHAIRMAN, INTEL

The best way to experience the power of fundamental choices is to make them.

—ROBERT FRITZ, AUTHOR,
THE PATH OF LEAST RESISTANCE

Organization and Resources: Essential Management Decisions

Developing a truly new business concept is difficult because it necessarily involves addressing many interrelated uncertainties. The early literature in innovation management, largely focused on technology, pointed out that a breakthrough in the lab did not ensure commercial success. It was equally important to shape the technical discovery in such a way that, when it was realized as a product or service, it created sufficient value in the market to justify its often relatively high costs—costs that were routinely underestimated.

In other words, to be successful, companies needed to resolve market uncertainties as well as technical uncertainties. In which markets would the new technology bring the greatest added value? What do these markets really need, and what would customers in those markets be willing to pay? Market uncertainties such as these often proved to be more difficult to resolve than the technical uncertainties that could be resolved in the laboratory.

In extreme cases, a new business concept might disrupt a market or be new to the world, making customer and market reactions unpredictable. In photography, for instance, it was clear that cameras using digital technology would eventually advance to the point that their picture quality would be comparable with (if not better than) that of standard film. That was predictable. What was not predictable was that millions of people who had never used a film camera would start to use digital cameras. Digital cameras became a standard addition to cellular phones. These were entirely new markets. A company working in digital camera technology would have had a very difficult time anticipating and forecasting demand for such new applications.

Even in less extreme cases, where market needs and customer demand could be reasonably forecast, large companies continued to experience difficulties in moving innovative developments to market. Researchers and observers of corporate entrepreneurship efforts recognized that technical and market uncertainties alone did not capture the full breadth of the new business creation problem in large organizations. The new technology underlying an innovative product might be proven and its intended marketplace correctly targeted, and yet the project might still fail. Often the concepts did come to fruition, but not within the company sponsoring the new business development effort. Clearly, for large organizations, there were challenges in new business creation that were not captured by the technology/market framework.

The answer seemed to be, in the famous words of Walt Kelly's Pogo Possum, "We have met the enemy, and he is us!" In addition to overcoming technical challenges and market foibles, bringing new businesses to fruition requires overcoming the resistance engendered within the corporation. A new business, by its nature, involves doing things differently. But large corporations become large by focusing intensely on competencies that make the existing businesses competitive. New business development projects are competing for corporate resources, but they do not fit with the existing businesses. Why would a business unit take on the technical and market risks of a new business when there are other, better-understood opportunities for growing the existing business? Why would it risk not meeting this quarter's revenue and profit targets by spending time and money on a promising but unproven project that might not scale into a self-sustaining business for years? Why not instead stick with the sustained incremental improvements afforded by implementing such measures as statistical quality management or customer satisfaction surveys?

This was largely the answer for large corporations during the 1980s and early 1990s, as suggested at the beginning of Chapter 1. (See Appendix B for a brief history of corporate entrepreneurship.) However, a few pioneering companies realized that, in addition to the useful and profitable efforts in quality management and incremental new product innovation, organic growth through new business creation could also be an important contributor to corporate success. Indeed, as discussed in Chapter 2, they began to see innovation as fundamentally a new business design problem rather than just a new product development problem. And they realized that in addition to seeking out intrepid corporate mavericks who were willing to work against the system, they could potentially make new business creation a regular (if not predictable), managed process.

Among the four general types of uncertainty—technical, market, organizational, and resource—large enterprises faced a strategic choice with the latter two. Technical and market uncertainties would vary by the project. Dealing with a corporation's organizational realities and resource allocation are two factors that are under the direct control of management. These are the cardinal management choices in the design of corporate entrepreneurship programs.

The Four Models of Corporate Entrepreneurship

Organizational and resource uncertainties are the two key dimensions *under the control of management* that distinguish corporate entrepreneurship approaches. We frame the organizational uncertainty issue in terms of organizational ownership: Who, if anyone, within the firm has primary ownership of the creation of new businesses? Responsibility and accountability for new business creation can be focused in a designated group or groups, or it can be diffused across the organization. We frame the resource uncertainty issues in terms of resource authority: Is there money dedicated in advance to corporate entrepreneurship, or are new business concepts funded in an ad hoc manner through divisional or corporate budgets or "slush funds"?

Together, the two dimensions generate a matrix with four dominant models, as depicted in Figure 3-1: the *Opportunist* (diffused ownership and ad hoc resource allocation), the *Enabler* (diffused ownership and dedicated resources), the *Advocate*

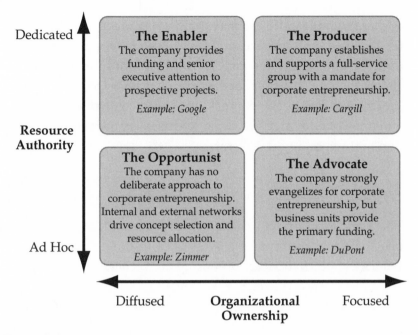

The Enabler
The company provides funding and senior executive attention to prospective projects.

Example: Google

The Producer
The company establishes and supports a full-service group with a mandate for corporate entrepreneurship.

Example: Cargill

The Opportunist
The company has no deliberate approach to corporate entrepreneurship. Internal and external networks drive concept selection and resource allocation.

Example: Zimmer

The Advocate
The company strongly evangelizes for corporate entrepreneurship, but business units provide the primary funding.

Example: DuPont

Dedicated

Resource Authority

Ad Hoc

Diffused   Organizational   Focused
Ownership

Figure 3-1

(focused ownership and ad hoc resource allocation), and the *Producer* (focused ownership and dedicated resources). Each model represents a distinct way of fostering corporate entrepreneurship. In the remainder of this chapter, we will describe each model and provide examples of companies that have adopted each approach. In Chapter 4, we will help you determine which model or models may be right for your company.

The Opportunist Model

All companies begin as Opportunists. Without any designated organizational ownership or resources, corporate entrepreneurship proceeds (if it does at all) based on the efforts and serendipity of intrepid "project champions"—people who toil against the odds, often creating new businesses in spite of the corporation (these are the mavericks we wrote about in Chapter 1). Small, entrepreneurial companies are Opportunists by their very nature. They are typically built around visionary champions and have leadership whose primary job is turning dreams into reality. Yet in large, established companies, encouraging visionaries and allocating sufficient management attention to these individuals is rare.

Zimmer: An Opportunist Model That Has Worked

There are some organizations in which innovative new business ideas may come from anywhere in the company, and there's a good chance that promising ones will get support and attention from top executives. Consider Zimmer, a medical device company founded in 1927 and headquartered in Warsaw, Indiana. Zimmer focuses on the design, development, manufacture, and marketing of reconstructive and spinal implants and trauma and related orthopedic surgical products. Zimmer has more than 8,500 employees in more than two dozen countries, with 2008 sales of about $4.1 billion. From 1972 to 2001, Zimmer was owned by Bristol Myers Squibb. It was spun off in August 2001, and Ray Elliott, president of the Zimmer subsidiary from 1997 to 2001, was named CEO of the independent company. (David C. Dvorak was appointed president and CEO of Zimmer on May 1, 2007.)

While Zimmer had been quite innovative during its time as a subsidiary, it began to flourish as an independent (but still large) company. Zimmer has R&D organizations that undertake new product development, but it has no formal organization or dedicated resources for corporate entrepreneurship. In the medical device field, innovative new business ideas often come from users. For instance, in 1997, trauma surgeon Dana Mears began experimenting with ideas for minimally invasive surgery for hip replacements. He presented the idea and explored it informally with Zimmer manager Kevin Gregg. While the product implications and business model for this approach were unclear, Mears received R&D funding to continue his exploratory work. By 2001, the procedure was ready for clinical trials. Mears and Gregg got the go-ahead to proceed from top management (including CEO Ray Elliott) and, more important, the go-ahead to develop the business approach to leverage this emerging new capability. Somehow, the improvement in surgical procedure—if significant—had to be turned into a competitive advantage for Zimmer.

The clinical trials revealed that the minimally invasive procedure could greatly improve patient outcomes, but there were many subtleties. To persuade surgeons to learn the procedure and begin to apply it preferentially—and therefore drive sales of implants and surgical tools—Zimmer conceived an innovative training program in order to accelerate learning. Surgeons who participated in training were required to share patient demographics, operative details, and complications for each of the first 10 procedures they performed after training, enabling new students to learn from their predecessors. In order to make the improvements in surgical performance ongoing, Zimmer established the Zimmer Institute in March 2003. The Zimmer Institute not only incorporated substantive training in minimally invasive procedures but, according to a 2005 Zimmer press release, also incorporated innovations in the training process itself, such as interactive online learning and virtual reality, as well as new educational techniques to address different learning styles and preferences. By 2006, more than 6000 surgeons had been trained there in a dozen different types of minimally invasive surgical procedures.

Not only has the Zimmer Institute developed a large coterie of surgeons who are trained in and comfortable with using

Zimmer hip replacement products, but the resulting improvement in patient outcomes created an innovative opportunity for Zimmer in the value capture dimension of new business design. Improved patient functionality and recovery times using the minimally invasive procedure meant lower total medical costs for hip and knee replacement procedures. These long-term savings allowed Zimmer to persuade certain private insurers to pay a premium for these procedures.

So what works at Zimmer? The essential element in the minimally invasive surgery example was a willingness to establish quasi-autonomous entrepreneurial teams to focus on the disruptive innovation, with top leadership support for investigating new ways of doing business. The concept was not subject to ordinary new product development processes or reviews, but rather was allowed to evolve on its own terms. This kind of flexibility was facilitated by the fact that Zimmer focuses on internal talent development and has many people in the ranks who have worked with the company for a decade or two. These veterans have learned how to find what they need around the organization, based on long-term relationships. They know how to move ideas forward based on informal communication and tacit approval. Finally, the U.S. medical device industry has been centered for many years in Warsaw, Indiana, creating a special industrial network in that area that over the years has maintained a delicate balance of collective support for the industry as a whole while engaging in intense competition within specific segments.

In general, the Opportunist Model works well only in trusting corporate cultures that are open to experimentation and that have diverse social networks behind the official hierarchy. In other words, there need to be multiple executives who can say yes to a new business concept. Without that type of environment, good ideas can easily fall through organizational cracks or receive insufficient funding to prove feasible. Clearly, such an environment can be hard to sustain; consequently, the Opportunist approach is not dependable for many companies in the long term. In some companies, an ad hoc innovation culture flows down from the very top and dissipates when a new CEO comes in. For other companies, their success in corporate entrepreneurship leads them to grow to a size where informal innovation management does not continue to work as well as it did when the company was smaller. Likewise, in some industries, the nature of competition may change from a locally dominated cluster to a globalized network in which an informal culture of innovation does not work reliably.

When organizations get serious about organic growth, executives realize that they need more than a diffused, ad hoc approach. For instance, Zimmer has instituted more formalized development practices for bringing new businesses to market, partly in response to the increasingly global nature of its business. It has instituted practices to synchronize the development of new technologies with the new product development projects in the company's development pipeline, so that there is a better flow of new technologies into new products and potentially new businesses. Scrutiny of the entire medical devices industry by the U.S. Department of Justice may make it difficult to maintain some of the informal communication and coordination practices that characterized industry competition in the past, which could lead to further changes in how Zimmer competes. As a result, while still fundamentally following the Opportunist Model, the company has begun to evolve beyond it.

The Enabler Model

When the Opportunist Model works, it does so because the corporate leadership culture values innovative new business creation and devotes time and energy to it. Therefore, a logical step for companies that are seeking to encourage corporate entrepreneurship is to create mechanisms for supporting employees and teams in conceiving new businesses and then systematically bringing these businesses to the attention of top management. This is the essence of the Enabler Model.

The basic premise of the Enabler Model is that employees across an organization will be willing and able to develop new business concepts if they are given adequate support and attention to lead them to believe that there is a good chance of the new business becoming real. Dedicating resources *enables* such teams to pursue opportunities largely on their own. Because there is no formal organizational ownership of such efforts, successful experiments or demonstrations depend on top management support if they are to be turned into new businesses. In this way, the Enabler Model is similar to the Opportunist Model, except that the early stages of new business conception are explicitly supported, encouraged, and often strategically channeled, with a promise of serious management attention to those concepts that look promising.

In rarer but very interesting cases, Enabler processes are employed as part of a broader, long-term plan to change the culture of an organization, that is, to transform a company without a strong tradition of innovation into one in which innovation and corporate entrepreneurship are encouraged and facilitated broadly throughout the organization. As noted in Chapter 1, undertaking broad cultural change requires a substantial and consistent commitment of top leadership, along with concomitant changes in many corporate management processes, from new product development processes to recruiting and human resources management. In this section, we will provide both an example of an inherently innovative organization that employs Enabler processes in order to enhance corporate entrepreneurship (Google) and a company without a tradition of innovation that employed such processes as part of a long-term plan to change the corporate culture (Whirlpool), with both core innovation and corporate entrepreneurship as objectives.

Google: An Ecosystem of Entrepreneurs

Google is the poster child for the Enabler Model. Google's innovations in Internet search and advertising have made its Web site a top Internet destination and its brand one of the most recognized in the world. Google maintains the world's largest online index of Web sites and other content. Google generates revenue by delivering targeted, online advertising and by licensing its advertising program to thousands of third-party Web sites. Founded in 1998 by Larry Page and Sergey Brin, building on three years of research as computer science Ph.D. candidates at Stanford University, the company has grown to more than 20,000 employees as of this writing. Revenues have grown from under $500,000 in 2002 to almost $22 billion in 2008.

Despite its tremendous growth and significant size today, Google maintains the open and freewheeling stance of a much smaller company. Keval Desai, a Google program manager, describes his company in the following way: "We're really an internal ecosystem of entrepreneurs . . . sort of like the [Silicon] Valley ecosystem but inside one company." At Google, employees are allowed to spend 20 percent of their time promoting their ideas to colleagues, assembling teams, exploring concepts, and building prototypes. Project groups form on the fly, based on requirements that are defined by the teams themselves. As a result, a project's initial success depends on the entrepreneurial capabilities of the project champion or champions. An initial core team typically includes a project manager, a technical lead, a product marketing manager (for competitive analyses, focus groups, market targeting, and so on), a user-interface designer, a quality-assurance specialist, and an attorney (for privacy, trademark, and other legal input).

If a project team believes that it has a winner, it appeals to the Google Product Council for formal project funding. The Product Council, which includes the company founders, top executives, and engineering team leaders, provides broad strategic direction and initial resources. The Product Council meets weekly to hear new business ideas. Successful project teams can receive assistance from the Google Product Strategy Forum to formulate a business model and set milestones. At this early stage, however, Google applies no preconceived criteria or hurdle rates to the projects. As long as a project appears to have potential and maintains the interest of Google employees, it can continue. The potential to profitably leverage Google's core— search, advertising, and channel partners—is typically not the first criterion applied to new business concepts. Of course, the notion that "Yahoo! might do it" provides added impetus for Google to try new things, as the Internet industry is changing constantly and remains highly competitive.

Only after a team successfully proves the technical aspects of an idea and demonstrates consumer interest does Google focus on how the firm's core elements might be leveraged to enable the emerging business model. At this point, the Google Product Strategy Forum may begin to play a more active oversight and support role, including obtaining more significant resources, directing formal and regular engineering reviews, acquiring outside capabilities, or making some other part of Google work with the project team. On occasion, the Google Product Strategy Forum will ask a project team to report to it; for example, if a competitor launches a new offering in the space, Google top executives will often want to maintain closer involvement in what Google is doing.

At any given time, Google is typically supporting more than 100 new business concepts in various stages of development, and information about the projects is maintained in a central, searchable database. Managers estimate that approximately 70 percent of the projects support the company's core business in some fashion, 20 percent represent emerging business ideas, and 10 percent are pursuing speculative experiments. In the early stages, an experimental Web page will typically be launched at a special labs.google.com Web site. Later, the team may set up its own page, for example, maps.google.com. For business concepts related to existing Google offerings, the VP under whose purview the concept falls will keep track of all research activity worldwide and seek to provide some strategic coherence to the overall corporate effort. If successful, a project or set of projects may be brought together to become, in effect, its own division. A special committee determines the very few businesses that may have a link on Google's primary consumer Web page, www.google.com.

If a project succeeds, team members can receive substantial bonuses (called Founders' Awards), sometimes amounting to millions of dollars. These bonuses do not match what entrepreneurs *might* make if they were successful on their own, but most employees see the benefits of remaining within Google—in particular, a much higher probability of success. Many Google managers have experience on the "outside" and thus relish the intense yet supportive and trusting atmosphere that Google offers.

Whirlpool: Building an Innovation Culture

Google's entrepreneurial culture, dynamic market, and extraordinary access to capital make the company's success difficult to replicate. Nonetheless, other companies have had success using the Enabler Model. Boeing, for example, has found that dedicated funds for innovation combined with clear, disciplined processes for allocating those funds can go a long way toward unlocking latent entrepreneurial potential. Well-designed Enabler practices also have the side benefit of exposing senior management to ambitious, innovative employees, allowing the company to identify and nurture future growth leaders.

Whirlpool is an interesting and unusual case, in that it began its corporate entrepreneurship journey from a baseline that was considered almost noninnovative. Over the course of about a decade, beginning in 1999, Whirlpool transformed itself from a conservative company in a slow-moving, commodity business into a creative engine spawning significant new revenues from differentiated products and new businesses. Whirlpool's transformation has been well documented, most recently in the 2008 book *Unleashing Innovation* by Nancy Tennant Snyder, who was charged with spearheading the change. We will not repeat the story here, but rather will highlight the essential Enabler elements of the process described in her book. In doing so, we will take a somewhat different stance on the case. Snyder highlighted the creativity unleashed by changing the culture of Whirlpool. Here, we focus on themes that are critical to ongoing corporate entrepreneurship: strategy, resource allocation, and executive engagement.

As we have emphasized several times already—and will continue to do as we move forward—the shift toward an ongoing corporate entrepreneurship effort should begin with a careful strategic assessment, so that innovation efforts can be focused. (Snyder begins one of her chapters with a quote by David Allen: "It is hard to be fully creative without constraint. Try painting without a canvas.") Dave Whitwam, who was then CEO, believed that Whirlpool could gain sustainable competitive advantage in the "white goods" industry (i.e., large appliances) by innovating fairly close to its core, focusing on new and compelling solutions to overlooked or unarticulated customer needs. He called this a Brand-Focused Value Creation Strategy. In the parlance of the Innovation Radar in Chapter 2, we would identify the focus as solutions, customer experience, and brand. Consistent with these points of emphasis, there would also be an emphasis on creating new platforms.

In the highly competitive white goods industry, the key to sustainable competitive advantage would be setting a new pace of innovation for the industry. This is what drove Whirlpool to undertake an ambitious program to embed innovative thinking and participation throughout the company rather than setting up a separate group charged with reinvigorating existing product lines or exploiting "white space" opportunities in areas that fell between the market or customer focus of existing business units. (We'll consider corporate entrepreneurship models that are appropriate for those objectives shortly.) "Innovation will come from everywhere and everyone, and when we are successful, every job at Whirlpool will change," Snyder quotes Whitwam as saying.

Whirlpool engaged in a wide variety of training programs and instituted several new management processes in order to transform itself. It created new processes for product development, personnel evaluation, knowledge management, financial accounting, and, most important for our purposes, resource allocation and project reviews. For early-stage funding, Whirlpool set up "seed funds." Whitwam mandated that Whirlpool's business units and regional offices spend a certain amount on supporting new concept development. He also maintained his own corporate seed funds, which he would use to fund worthy ideas that had been rejected by business units or regional offices. (Interestingly, according to Snyder, the

CEO's strong direction and personal interest was sufficient to make business units and regional offices attentive to new ideas; he rarely had to use corporate funds.) Midstage funding for innovation or corporate entrepreneurship projects was controlled primarily by new oversight and review bodies known as I-boards. I-boards consisted of business leaders of various types. Some were populated by senior executives, others by product teams, business unit leadership, or brand teams. I-boards created multiple executives who could say yes to a new business concept, which, as noted earlier, is a key element of an Opportunist culture that Enabler processes seek to exploit. People with innovative project concepts are free to shop their ideas around to different I-boards for funding.

The key change that made all of this work was a top-level set-aside of a fixed percentage of the capital expenditure budget for innovation projects. To make this incentive even more salient, business units that did not generate enough worthy innovation or corporate entrepreneurship concepts would see their allocation of capital funds reduced. This set up an internal competition for new ideas. Dedicated resources were a key component of making the innovation program successful.

By 2006, Whirlpool's transformation effort was bearing significant fruit. The company tracks innovation projects carefully after launch. In 2006, these projects created $1 billion of new revenues, out of a total of about $18 billion. In 2007, that figure rose to $2.7 billion out of $19.4 billion. In 2008, it was $4 billion out of $19 billion. Growing revenues from innovation are allowing Whirlpool to maintain its top-line corporate revenue level, despite a significant drop in the housing market and a broad overall recession.

Whirlpool's accomplishments are impressive, but it is important to emphasize the depth and persistence of senior executive commitment required to make it happen. As noted in Chapter 1, seeking cultural change can doom corporate entrepreneurship efforts. A reviewer of the Whirlpool experience (quoted by Snyder) noted, "One way to think of Whirlpool Corporation would be as an appliance company that is innovative. But a better characterization might be that Whirlpool has become an innovation center that makes appliances." We've heard this before from other companies. One told us that it wanted to become an innovative company that makes furniture, as opposed to an innovative furniture company. This is usually a mistake. Indeed, we would argue that Whirlpool's success is due precisely to the fact that it had a well-thought-out strategy that was attuned to its deep knowledge of its core business. We are currently working with a company in the defense industry that is interested in enhancing its corporate entrepreneurship performance. While enhancing the innovation potential embedded in its experienced workforce will be part of the corporate entrepreneurship program, we are suggesting that culture change not be announced as an explicit objective, but rather be done quietly, beginning around the edges and then moving toward the core slowly and organically. As noted in Chapter 1, trying to make everybody innovative is usually not the right way for companies in this position to proceed.

Even in Whirlpool's case, evolution of its model toward a greater focus on corporate entrepreneurship rather than other forms of innovation may be warranted. To qualify as an innovation project, an idea must be new to the world, not just new to Whirlpool, and it must not be able to be copied by competitors. Yet having changed the corporate culture in ways that permit opportunistic innovation, there may be ways for Whirlpool to leverage its brand in areas where competition exists, as well as to profit from opportunities further out from its core. For instance, Su Yong and Chen Xiaoping reported in *Comprehensive Research on Brands* how Haier of China discovered an agricultural application for its clothes washers by taking a creative turn on a customer service problem among its rural customers. Haier clothes washers were being returned by rural customers because of clogging of the water pipes. When customer service representatives were sent out to investigate, they discovered that farmers were using the machines to clean root vegetables. With a few simple adjustments, Haier launched a successful product aimed at that market, aptly named Big Yam. Big Yam, which has become a bestseller, is generating revenue in an area that would be easy to copy technically, but in which Haier has created brand equity that is not so easy to displace. Whirlpool might be able to discover similar opportunities if it broadened its scope.

As the Google and Whirlpool examples illustrate, the Enabler Model is not just about allocating capital for corporate entrepreneurship. Personnel development and executive engagement are also critical. The Enabler Model assumes that there are ample good ideas around the company and, more important, that there are individuals and teams that are interested and willing to flesh them out. Recruiting and retention of people who have entrepreneurial dispositions—but who can and want to operate within a large company—are essential. Google, for instance, spends an extraordinary amount of time and effort on recruiting. To be hired, a program manager or senior engineering candidate might go through 20 interviews in multiple stages before the company determines whether that individual has the right combination of "entrepreneurial DNA," broad technical talent, and intellectual agility. In the Whirlpool case, a bold multiyear initiative brought forward the latent creativity of employees steeped in the culture and history of what was otherwise a staid and stable industry.

Executive engagement is also essential if people are to trust that the company is committed to turning good and proven concepts into real businesses. Without sufficient support from senior management, promising concepts can end up as casualties of conflicts with established businesses. If senior executives are not committed to using Enabler processes to investigate and develop truly new businesses, then funding provided for projects can degenerate into "bowling for dollars"—simply an alternative source of funds for ordinary business unit projects or for projects that the company is not particularly serious about. In the most evolved versions of the Enabler Model, companies provide clear criteria for selecting which opportunities to pursue, guidelines for applying for funding, decision-making transparency, and, perhaps above all, well-defined engagement from senior management. Whirlpool was particularly sensitive to the "bowling for dollars" problem. What qualified as an innovative project for the purposes of receiving an allocation from the capital budget— recall there was a fixed percentage set aside for innovative projects—was carefully defined and monitored.

The selection criteria for project funding can serve as an important expression of corporate strategic intent. In some cases, there may be significant benefits to mine from cross-divisional collaboration. In other cases, a company may want to encourage innovation in the spaces between businesses or by taking divisional capabilities into entirely new markets. Providing such strategic direction may deter corporate entrepreneurship in certain business dimensions, but if it is well designed, it should encourage a critical mass of effort in those areas that are deemed most important to the company's future. The importance of focusing innovation efforts is suggested by a 2007 McKinsey Global Survey of top managers ("How Companies Approach Innovation"), which found it to be the most common type of engagement leaders have in the innovation processes of their company (more common than, for instance,

determining the overall innovation budgets or go/no-go decisions on specific innovation projects).

The Advocate Model

The Advocate Model represents another way in which companies can evolve beyond being Opportunists. In some corporate
cultures, business units enjoy significant autonomy from the
corporate core. In such an environment, a new business opportunity must, as a practical matter, be adopted by a business unit
in order to come to fruition. This does not mean, however, that
business units are left on their own to develop new businesses.
In the Advocate Model, a company assigns organizational ownership for driving the creation of new businesses to a designated corporate-level group, but it intentionally provides the
group with only a modest budget. Advocate organizations act
as evangelists and innovation experts, facilitating corporate
entrepreneurship in conjunction with business units, which
must demonstrate their commitment to new business development by paying most of the bills.

The Advocate Model is a relatively new and in some ways
counterintuitive form of corporate entrepreneurship. A primary purpose of contemporary corporate entrepreneurship
efforts is to overcome the resistance of business units to adopting immature new business concepts. So how can an organization that has no direct power over business units accomplish
very much? In some corporate contexts, it cannot. But, surprisingly, in many corporate contexts, it can.

We provide two examples here: DuPont, the 200-year-old
global conglomerate famous for its inventions in advanced
materials, and BP, the U.K.-based international oil giant.
DuPont was a pioneer in this method of new business creation.
At BP, an advocate-style organization drives IT-based trans-

formation across the company. Both share the essential aspect of not having a significant budget for new business creation. Instead, they work in a decentralized fashion to help business units either create new businesses or transform how they approach the businesses in which they currently operate. In this second case, the company is, in effect, undertaking corporate entrepreneurship in the sense that BP's advocate-style organization works with business units to innovate their business systems in meaningful ways.

DuPont: Market-Driven Innovation

In 1999, CEO Chad Holliday of DuPont realized that the company needed some new thinking because, even though margins and returns had improved during the prior six years, growth had declined. The company was growing its earnings largely through cost reductions rather than by increasing top-line revenues. So Holliday asked senior executives in the corporate plans group to delve into strategic options for generating greater organic top-line growth. DuPont veteran Robert A. Cooper headed the effort.

DuPont's primary businesses revolved around advanced materials. Over time, these materials would become commoditized, driving down margins. Also, the process of moving new materials from the lab to the market often involved numerous fits and starts. Cooper came to the conclusion that DuPont's effort to derive higher margins needed more "knowledge-intensive" products. The company needed to go "beyond the molecule." In other words, rather than continuing to focus on generating new products in its existing markets, DuPont needed to generate new businesses that leveraged the company's prodigious R&D inventiveness but provided additional value from its knowledge of working with new materials.

Cooper and two DuPont staffers sought out academic and other insights into how to drive new business development. At the time, there was not much of a literature, as DuPont was among the first companies to think seriously about corporate entrepreneurship as a driver of organic growth. The company needed to determine what would be the practices and principles of a corporate-level effort that would work for DuPont. Cooper partnered with a range of thought leaders, including Ian MacMillan, Rita Gunther McGrath, and Adrian Slywotzky, to design a high-level program concept incorporating the latest insights and procedures for generating and building new businesses.

After incorporating lessons learned from a pilot program, the ultimate result was the DuPont Market-Driven Innovation (MDI) initiative. MDI is a five-stage process. Underlying each of the phases is a comprehensive set of methodologies and frameworks that supports the teams and provides consistency and rigor to the process. The essential first stage is Leadership Framing, during which the MDI team works with business unit leadership to define the core mission, growth domain, and decision criteria for opportunities that they are willing to fund. The core mission refers to the maximum value proposition for customers and society, a lofty definition that allows the team to cast a broad but relevant net. The growth criteria define the factors that the leadership will use to select opportunities. The growth domains articulate areas for potential growth that satisfy the mission and rate well against the growth criteria. These sessions don't define the new business concept, but they make it clear to everyone where the business unit is willing to play, and under what conditions. "We wouldn't even begin a project without top business unit leadership spending an intense two days with us developing and articulating the strategic vision and operating boundaries," says Cooper.

The next stage of the MDI program is aimed at conceptualizing new business ideas that are consistent with the strategic framing. A four-day "business builder" session helps people from both inside and outside DuPont generate and prioritize different business concepts. Teams will then typically spend between four and eight weeks developing a detailed business plan, including a 180-day contract with senior management to address major uncertainties of any concepts that are deemed promising enough to justify such an effort. The process brings to the surface not only opportunities to innovate business system components but also gaps in the company's existing capabilities. The team and a facilitator from the MDI program will present the plan to business unit leadership for approval and next-stage funding.

If the project is funded, the team moves into the concept validation phase. Unlike initial business conception, which is typically qualitative and somewhat abstract, concept validation is much more data-driven. Here, teams pursue their 180-day contract with senior management, managing business risk by spending minimal resources in the early phases to test uncertainties and validate or invalidate their initial insights in real market environments. A concept can be canceled at any point in the process; however, most often the process brings uncertainties to the surface and tests hypotheses in ways that help new business design teams evolve the concept for successful commercialization during the Execute phase. As the concept matures, MDI applies a process known as Discovery-Driven Planning, a rigorous approach to tying uncertainty resolution to actions and learning objectives described by Rita Gunther McGrath and Ian MacMillan in a 1995 *Harvard Business Review* article.

The core of the MDI program had only about half a dozen full-time employees, and becoming part of that group was a sought-after opportunity for up-and-coming managers who wanted to gain senior-level exposure and have a direct impact on the company's growth. The best advocates come from a company's veteran ranks—those who are well known, respected, and experienced in making change happen within the organization. As Cooper recalls, "I thought I'd spend most of my time helping design and build new businesses. . . . Instead, I spent at least half my time advocating."

Success within one business unit has a way of building interest from others, and over time, teams like those at DuPont can become critical change agents. Although DuPont's senior executives actively and openly support the program, they have never mandated its adoption by the company's different business units. In 1999, DuPont's corporate headquarters invested in the process development and the pilot engagements to allow the program to gain credibility, but after that, each business unit had to pay its own way. Today, there is still no requirement that business units participate, but they do so because they recognize the value of the program. One of the program's early supporters was Ellen Kullman, then group vice president for DuPont's Safety and Protection businesses, who has since become a big champion of the initiative. By 2005, Kullman noted, "We have nearly a half a billion dollars of new revenues we would not have had had it not been for this program." Partly as a result of her success at driving organic growth within her business unit, Kullman ascended to become DuPont's CEO in January 2009.

BP: Office of the CTO

BP, the U.K.-based oil giant, provides a distinct example of the Advocate Model of corporate entrepreneurship. In 2001, the Office of the Chief Technology Officer (CTO) for Digital and Communications Technology—which reported to the chief information officer (CIO) for the entire company—was tasked with finding ways to significantly transform BP's various businesses using emerging information technologies (IT). The late 1990s had seen a massive consolidation of the oil industry. BP was a leader of that trend, and by 2001, the company consisted of 130 business units with about 100,000 employees in more than 100 countries. Although the extensive merger activity had been driven by low oil prices, BP's CEO, Lord Browne of Madingley, anticipated significant learning across business units, what he called "intellectual economies of scale." Browne saw IT "not just as a service function but as an activity which could change the nature of the business itself."

Lord Browne turned to his CIO, John Leggate, and Leggate's right-hand man, the vice president of IT integration, Phiroz P. Darukhanavala, known to everyone as "Daru." Daru was tasked with designing an organization, which he would then lead, to drive significant, IT-based business innovation and value within BP's operating businesses. He quickly decided that the business transformation function should not be appended to mainstream IT groups, as they needed to stay focused on maintaining the company's applications, networks, data centers, backbones, and so on. Indeed, he concluded that any large internal organization would be too slow and prone to ossifying around a few big projects. Such a group would also not fit well with BP's independent business unit organization and culture.

After considering many models, Daru focused on how venture capital groups operated. These were small organizations, although nevertheless well informed. They became well informed not by maintaining extensive in-house expertise but rather by developing networks that allowed them to find solutions quickly. In project management, they could orchestrate small teams and move very nimbly. Over time, Daru concluded that his new organization—the CTO office, with him as CTO—

should be a small, technically strong team that was well informed about BP business unit needs and highly networked with external companies and experts across the global IT ecosystem. Its operating focus would be on bringing in new digital technology from the outside to improve the company's operations and performance in areas beyond the traditional IT domains of transaction processing and enterprise resource planning.

Unlike a venture capital organization, however, Daru did something counterintuitive. He requested a modest budget—about $10 million out of BP's $2.5 billion IT budget—and no formal authority. He reasoned that in BP's culture, a central group with a large budget would foster resistance and become disconnected from the business units. Having limited resources would require that business units fund implementation projects, which would help ensure that the CTO office's activities made business sense rather than becoming just research-type activities. The CTO office would be measured by how much bottom-line value it delivered through persuading businesspeople with profit-and-loss responsibilities. The CTO office's job would be to perform due diligence on external firms and develop concepts with them that were relevant to BP's business units. The CTO office would then act as matchmakers, coaches, and translators, bridging the significant cultural and operational gaps between small technology firms and a large global enterprise like BP. As part of this process, it would often have to bridge groups within BP that otherwise might not connect.

Daru founded the CTO office with six carefully selected professionals. He then slowly built the group to just over a dozen people, which is where it stands today. Fewer would be insufficient to generate and manage a critical mass of projects; more would require too much administration and coordination. He was highly selective in hiring—only one person out of every ten or more serious candidates received an offer. It sometimes took the better part of a year to make a hire. Daru wanted people with a strong background in IT technologies, but not with in-depth expertise in any one. These people were not expected to be the sources of new technology. Instead, they would need to be able to interact with the broad IT ecosystem, develop an overview of a given area, and quickly understand the trade-offs among the available options. He also wanted most of the people reporting to him to have experience in a business area of BP: exploration, oil and gas production, refining, retail marketing, or some other area. Ideally, he wanted to have at least one person from each major BP business area. About a quarter of the team would be outside hires, bright people in an IT field with at least 20 years of significant experience. They would learn the oil business at BP.

The early years of the CTO office were characterized by experimentation and learning as it defined its roles and processes in connecting the external IT ecosystem with internal BP business unit needs. The team initiated relationships with IT suppliers, research firms, consultants, academics, venture capitalists, government agencies, industry groups, and major customers. Relationship building with the ecosystem was critical, as the CTO office could not drive IT-based innovation without knowing the IT industry pipeline. The CTO office discovered that these external players were typically happy to engage with BP, as the company provided a "real-world" opportunity for vendors to apply their products and build relationships with BP's internal experts. For its part, the CTO office committed to arriving at its decisions quickly and providing constructive feedback if the projects did not go forward, which stands in stark contrast to the typically complex, time-consuming negotiations with many other large, global companies.

At the same time, the CTO office also had to begin engaging senior BP leadership; it was committed to doing more than just "pushing" technology solutions to business units. Rather, it had to articulate the value proposition for BP and demonstrate what the technology could contribute in a real business application. Focusing from the start on articulating real business value was critical to building credibility and a reputation among the business units. One method of engagement came to be known as Blue Chalk events. Blue Chalk events are small seminars that expose BP leadership to the potential business significance of emerging IT. The CTO office tries to have at least one senior executive cosponsor each event, which focuses on a particular theme. These events serve as a seeding process for new ideas and a forum for seeking management alignment around a particular topic by exposing multiple external viewpoints or approaches.

In the early years, projects would generally begin by identifying an emerging technology that met a business challenge and discussing it with relevant BP management. The CTO office would then scan its network for relevant offerings, quickly focusing on likely vendors. If a technology looked promising, the CTO office would recommend a small trial—perhaps $50,000, including management time—with a narrow scope and well-defined objectives. If the technology generally delivered what the vendors promised, then a larger-scale demonstration might be recommended as part of an overall rollout strategy. Responsibility for any rollout would be transitioned to the business unit, with the CTO office providing facilitation where necessary. The expectation was that full implementation of the technology would be supported by the business unit's budget. However, the CTO team built a reputation for being willing to iterate and endure where others were ready to drop an idea as soon as significant problems arose. What mattered was deploying successful projects, and that often depended on perseverance. That being said, "We don't get bogged down," explains Daru. "The process is designed to remove the 'clutter' . . . [and] identify really significant opportunities." In its relationships with the business units, "We go where the energy is. We don't fight battles."

Focusing on project transition to business units could lead the CTO group to become too timid in its project goals. To counter this, starting in 2003, it initiated annual Game Changer initiatives: innovative programs with significant transformative potential and at least $50 to $100 million of expected bottom-line impact. Game Changer projects go through three stages that each last about a year: (1) ideation and evangelization, (2) pilots and scale-up, and (3) transition to business units. By 2005, the CTO office had three Game Changers running concurrently. During the ideation and evangelization stage, the CTO staff undertakes a complete market analysis, looking at every entity it can identify that is involved in the technology. The staff members talk to end users, locate executives at other companies who are willing to discuss the benefits and costs of implementation, and visit technology providers and research groups. The CTO office then conducts proof-of-concept tests with the business to ascertain whether the technology can be expected to achieve the value propositions hypothesized for BP. To date, all but one Game Changer have been pursued to a successful outcome.

Many BP executives were initially skeptical about the role and potential impact of a small group like the CTO office. As business successes mounted, skepticism gave way to support, and the office's brand and impact grew. Based on its reputation for solving problems (without becoming too caught up in bureaucratic processes), the CTO office began receiving unprompted questions from business unit managers. It increasingly came to be perceived as a strategic contributor to BP business units.

In 2006, the team formalized a more business-led process into what became known as Business Unit Partnering. Business Unit Partnering engages business unit leaders early, obtaining sponsorship for workshops focused on what they believe to be their most pressing challenges. In other words, "needs pull" from business units has become a more explicit focus (rather than "pushing" emerging technologies at business unit problems). Business Unit Partnering begins with each CTO senior staff member connecting with carefully selected business units, with the goal of developing a detailed understanding of their challenges. Using connections within the business units developed during previous engagements, the CTO office works with staff members to identify pressing challenges, highlighting past technology successes and seeding the discussion with preliminary ideas for innovative, nontraditional digital solutions. Next, Daru and key CTO team members meet with the business unit leader and his or her leadership team to define the highest-priority performance and operational problems facing their business unit.

Each business unit engagement presents its own challenges. With some, it's budget allocation. With others, it's focus and follow-through. The higher level of visibility puts additional pressure on the CTO office to maintain its reputation for delivering solid business value. The team has also discovered that the timing and risk tolerance for the adoption of even proven technologies differ among business units. The CTO office has begun to keep track of different business units' timing for a better sense of when and how to feed prospects to new business unit partners.

This transition to a more needs-oriented or market-focused perspective—rather than a technology or product/offering focus—is characteristic of many of the structured corporate entrepreneurship efforts that we've observed. Staying focused on business adoption, rather than technical impressiveness, is an important discipline. It is essential to the Advocate Model, where a primary concern is finding which avenues of adoption within a business unit will have the best chance of working.

Keep in mind that Advocate organizations cannot compel business units to do anything, and they are, by design, unable to pursue projects themselves beyond initial concept development and due diligence. Their power rests in their ability to educate, connect, and persuade.

In order to broker connections for business units, an Advocate organization must first make and maintain those connections itself. It must build knowledge and trust among both internal networks and the external ecosystem. Recall the quote from Professor Andrew Hargadon in the introduction: "Pursuing a strategy of technology brokering means recognizing that a key role of corporate R&D is bridging the many different industries and markets that exist, and building the necessary combinations of technologies and people to make potential breakthroughs possible."

Advocate organizations must also tend to their own corporate-level viability by maintaining awareness and support among corporate leadership. Of course, testimonials from business unit leadership about bottom-line results are most persuasive. But Advocate organizations can also reassure the top leaders that the company is being exposed to leading-edge thinking and technologies. More important, a well-staffed Advocate team can sort "the wheat from the chaff" in emerging technologies, where visions are often quite different from substance.

For Advocate organizations that are focused on bringing emerging external technologies to bear on business unit problems, their primary role is to serve as a translator between the priorities of the (usually) small firm and those of a large corporation, helping to overcome what can otherwise tend to be a fundamental mismatch for many small-to-large-corporation negotiations. Small firms are often eager to display their capabilities to a major potential customer, and the large company can gain a competitive advantage by serving as the proving ground for a company and technology that are on the brink of achieving market success. But the negotiations can be delicate, involving such things as intellectual property protection and ownership. On the other hand, the large company can be more than just a major customer. It can often help to develop a market by bringing together several component part suppliers to achieve a system solution.

A fundamental challenge for Advocate organizations is to maintain a balance between explorations of longer-term, game-changing concepts and producing tangible near-term results. It takes time to fill the pipeline, and individual projects may have a long gestation period.

Another challenge is to remain current, not only in understanding the external ecosystem but also in employing leading-edge methods and practices in corporate entrepreneurship. Good Advocate teams are introspective and regularly seek outside process concepts and advice. DuPont's Advocate group has changed its basic operating motif three times since 1999. In 2006, BP's CTO group was challenged by a corporate advisory group not to rest on its laurels. So it applied to itself the same approach that it used for concept development: going out to its network for advice and leading-edge thinking on the process of being an Advocate organization. Business Unit Partnering was one of the new approaches that came out of these investigations, as well as the addition of modern, Internet-mediated methods for building external networks of concept developers and solutions providers, such as NineSigma.Com, InnoCentive.Com, and yet2.com.

The Producer Model

A few companies, such as Cargill, Cisco, and IBM, pursue corporate entrepreneurship by establishing and supporting formal organizations with significant dedicated funds or significant influence over business unit funding. Setting up a separate, empowered organization—which we classify broadly as the Producer Model—is a common suggestion in the current corporate innovation literature. The Producer Model aims to protect emerging projects from turf battles, to encourage cross-unit collaboration, to build potentially disruptive businesses, and to create pathways for executives to pursue careers outside their business units. Unlike the separate organizations of the 1970s and 1980s, however, current implementations are conscious of the difficulties that such separated organizations have traditionally had in bringing proven new businesses back into the mainstream company. They are more than privileged versions of central R&D. Modern Producer organizations are closely tied to corporate leadership and strategy, and they provide a great deal of support for the commercialization, transition, and scaling of new businesses.

Cargill: Emerging Business Accelerator

Cargill, the privately held, $75 billion global agriculture products and services company, established its Emerging Business Accelerator (EBA) in 2001 to pursue corporate entrepreneurship. EBA is not about innovation, per se. Cargill has a chief innovation officer organization, embedded within Product Development, that focuses on developing ideas for innovation that can potentially be applied in other parts of the company. Cargill made a conscious decision to separate this innovation promotion function, which focuses on tools, processes, and other enhancements to existing businesses, from EBA, which is about building new businesses. As David Patchen, the group's founder and managing director, recalls, "Prior to the EBA, we lacked a clearly defined process for pursuing opportunities that fell outside of the scope of existing business units and functions. . . . We needed a new approach to complement our business units and Cargill Ventures [an internal venture group]."

One of the first questions in setting up the EBA was where it should look for opportunities. Cargill decided to stay within the agriculture and food supply chain, but that's a large space. Indeed, expanding into new business areas related to agriculture has been a hallmark of Cargill's growth. Its founding business was a grain storage elevator near a railroad track, then the company began transporting grain, then it began trading commodities, then it went into the primary transformation businesses (e.g., turning soybeans into protein, oils, and so on), which led into businesses such as animal feed and basic food supplies. Nevertheless, at Cargill and elsewhere, existing business unit managers often don't know what to do with new concepts that don't fit their business, and management incentives typically discourage them from absorbing near-term losses.

That's where the Emerging Business Accelerator comes in. Cargill believed that many new business opportunities were not being pursued because of a lack of fit within existing businesses, a higher risk profile, or unfocused attention. It wanted to shorten the cycle time it was taking to generate new businesses. Prior to the EBA, new ventures were run by people who were already running other businesses. It was seen as important that new business development projects be pursued by full-time, independent teams. EBA was created in 2004 for the following purposes:

- To be a global clearinghouse to originate value propositions, that is, a place for people to send their new business ideas
- To focus on opportunities that will generate revenues within three years (so that people would not think of EBA as an R&D funding source)

- To select, staff, fund, and monitor—but not operate—a portfolio of new businesses (EBA is not expected to act as a project manager)
- To graduate successful businesses into the world of Cargill

For instance, when Cargill's deicing business unit identified a novel deicing technology, the group realized that it might not be well suited to develop and commercialize the innovation. The technology—an epoxy overlay that inhibits ice formation—was going be a high-end product that would be sold to road builders worldwide for critical applications such as bridges. But Cargill's deicing business unit primarily sells commodity products to Department of Transportation agencies in North America. So the new technology was transferred to the Emerging Business Accelerator, which brought the offering to market.

Successes such as this have helped the Emerging Business Accelerator achieve its goal of being a global clearinghouse for new concepts and value propositions across Cargill. The group maintains a Web site for people to submit ideas, from both inside and outside the company. The project selection process generally proceeds as follows:

- *Origination.* EBA asks four basic questions in the early stages of a business concept: (1) What is the idea? (2) What is the value to the customer? (3) What is the value to Cargill? (4) What are the points of differentiation and the competitive advantage?
- *Preliminary due diligence (15 days).* This involves an initial market assessment of the broad financial parameters of the marketplace. Is it a growth market? What is the competitive landscape? This is not an assessment of the economics of the new business concept, as this would be premature and could suck the life out of it too early.

Rather, it's an assessment of the marketplace potential and the economics of the market.

- *Due diligence (next 60–90 days).* The EBA team conducts a typical due diligence process prior to submitting an investment memo to its board. If the investment is approved, EBA begins to implement a high-level plan, which includes the three most important questions about the concept—i.e., What are the most critical uncertainties?, How much money is it going to take to get there?, and How many people will be needed?
- *Recruit talent and provide funds (next 30 days).*
- *Monitor performance (next 1–5 years).* What is the progress in resolving the three critical uncertainties? If a project is not hitting its milestones, EBA revisits it. Perhaps these were not the correct three questions, and hence these were not the right milestones. Or maybe there are other learnings that are valuable.

Projects that achieve validation from real customers graduate into either existing or new business units. From a profit-and-loss standpoint, Cargill's structure is largely decentralized at the business unit level. Top-level corporate executives allocate capital and human resources and seek strategic synergies among business units. They can strongly influence which business unit should adopt a proven EBA business, based on which one has the appropriate go-to-market expertise, connections, channels, and so on. If necessary, top corporate executives can set up a new business unit to house the opportunity. At present, Cargill has about 80 business units organized around five platforms.

Through 2008, the EBA has evaluated more than 450 opportunities. It has invested in 13, of which 2 have "graduated" into ongoing Cargill businesses, 2 were sold, 4 were discontinued,

and 5 remain in the EBA portfolio. It employs many development paths: greenfield investments, patent licensing, minority
investments tied to business development agreements, and
small acquisitions. It selects, staffs, and monitors—but does not
operate—new business opportunities. In essence, it manages
the process but not the ideas, which helps build trust and
encourages collaboration among stakeholders.

Cisco: Emerging Markets Technology Group

Beginning in 2005, Cisco executives investigated and contem-
plated several trends in information technology that suggested
that the company would need to become much more engaged
in learning about and exploiting new business opportunities, not
just continued innovation in its core markets. The locus of innovation in the information technology industry was moving from
the enterprise space (e.g., e-business) to the consumer space.
Concurrently, just about everything seemed to be using Internet
protocols, so that anything that could be connected was becoming connected. Also, the Internet was moving from text-based to
video-based applications. By 2007, the amount of traffic consumed by consumers exceeded that consumed by businesses for
the first time, as a result of video. Five video sites in 2008 generated more traffic than the entire U.S. Internet in 2001, and all
of them had been created since 2004, within the past five years.

The rise of video provides an interesting window on future
information technology trends. Much of the video traffic today
is piracy. But this "subversive edge" is instructive, as it reflects
a real market need: people want the convenience of music and
video on demand. Every Internet-based service or content
provider is trying to stamp out the underlying peer-to-peer
protocols, but they just become more robust, more scalable, and
more bulletproof. But these same technologies could enable the

reinvention of television, as they permit you to download content from your neighbors without the need for a large content distribution network. Already today the BBC uses peer-to-peer networking to distribute some of its programming. The beauty of peer-to-peer technology is that the more customers there are, the faster the network works. So there is clearly a market opportunity there.

Cisco did not have a lot of experience back in 2005 with consumer markets. But Cisco knew that it needed to play here and in other emerging information technology markets in order to continue growing at a pace sufficient to maintain its stock value. The question was, how could Cisco take advantage of such trends? Acquisitions and partnerships, a Cisco strength, could certainly play a role. But in order to make acquisitions and partnerships most productive, Cisco would also need to begin building organic capabilities. It would need to become a real player and contributor in this space.

The answer for Cisco was to create a new organization called the Emerging Markets Technology Group (EMTG). EMTG's mission would be to detect important market trends while they were still nascent, conceive ways in which Cisco could take advantage of them, and organically grow new ventures inside the company. Cisco decided that a central group with a strong mandate would be required to defend corporate entrepreneurship projects against both corporate antibodies (the people who want to kill it before it gets started) and corporate love (the people who want to latch onto it and turn it toward their priorities). In looking at other companies, Cisco found no successful examples of decentralized new business incubation, so it decided that EMTG must have a budget for that. Finally, it was deemed important for a central group to be accountable for projects all the way to building and selling product, not just developing concepts for others to prove out.

Because Cisco is large, EMTG has to focus on large targets. Wall Street's expectations for growth presented top management with a $6.5 billion gap to fill in the next few years. So EMTG is looking for markets that can generate $1 billion annually within five to seven years. This has translated into launching 15 successful EMTG businesses, enough to spread risk and allow for variation in time to market, but not so many as to get dispersed. EMTG set itself a target of succeeding with three-quarters of its efforts, so this meant starting 20 projects during this period. EMTG believes that it can achieve this relatively high success ratio on large-scale projects by avoiding the problems that generally plague start-ups, such as the founder problem (great idea people who can't manage), running out of cash, being killed by bigger competitors, or having poor integration with products made by others.

Few initial ideas will make it through the various due diligence and market sizing investigations that make up the standard front end of a corporate entrepreneurship project. Perhaps no more than 1 in 50 ideas can be turned into large-scale concepts. So this meant that EMTG must bring in 1000 ideas or more for preliminary investigation. It started by canvassing its business partners, customers, and employees. EMTG started a wiki called iZone to gather these and developed a WebEx space for collaboration. This generated many dozens of ideas, but it was not enough. So EMTG created an incentive program called iPrize. The winner of an iPrize is personally awarded $250,000, and Cisco commits to invest at least $10 million in the concept. Two months after iPrize was launched, Cisco received more than 1200 ideas! Many of these 1200 ideas were not very good or very significant. But EMTG's attitude is that sometimes poorly thought out or small-scale ideas represent individual views of a big market opportunity. It may take a dozen ideas to flesh out a concept that represents an addressable and lucrative market opportunity.

To build integrated concepts, you need entrepreneurs. In many, if not most, companies, capable entrepreneurial project leaders—what DuPont came to call Business Builders—are a rare breed. Cisco was fortunate, however. EMTG looked around the corporation and discovered that more than half of the entrepreneurs in the start-up companies it had acquired over the past 10 years were still working at Cisco. When these entrepreneurs found out what EMTG was doing, they came knocking.

A typical project team will have a general manager, an engineering lead, a product development person, and a business development person. If the concept looks promising after initial investigations, it graduates to being a business, and it hires its own engineers. By the time the team has a product, there may be 50 or so people involved. In early market testing of the new product or system, EMTG is disciplined about selecting its customers. Early customers are viewed as development partners, not just potential sources of future revenue. Thus, they need to be chosen carefully to generate as much relevant market learning as possible. It often makes sense to select those customers whose problems are most compelling, which are not necessarily the same customers as those in the largest projected market segment. The most important thing *not* to do is to try to address all the potential markets at once. If you try to please everybody with your version 1.0 product, you will get bogged down.

If things are still looking good in market tests, then about six months before a full market launch, EMTG forms a "tiger team" of people from manufacturing, finance, service, sales, and other divisions to work out all the dependencies. These people meet every week to determine the go-to-market strategy. This is also the time when organizational conflicts are resolved, so that the transition from a proven technology and market into a scaling business does not falter, as is often the case during this critical and difficult transition.

It's important to realize that a project moves through different life cycles during this process, and the personnel have to be matched to this. Some people are great inventors; others are great evangelists; still others are great optimizers. Projects need to be run like a relay race, with the results being passed on to a different group as they reach the next stage of maturity. For inventors, you want people with passion, but also "coachability." If they are stubborn, they can kill projects—what we call "the founder's deadly embrace." In the next stage, you need great marketing people, like a Steve Jobs. In the final stage, you need great operational people, the kind who are running your business units today.

EMTG found that it was not necessary to create large financial incentives for its projects. You will encounter many people who want you to pay them up front for sharing their ideas. In fact, the best entrepreneurs tend to be the ones who are telling their ideas to everyone who will listen! Having separate financial incentives can disrupt internal equity in a company. (Even in freewheeling Google, this happens sometimes with its Founders' Awards.) Success has a thousand parents, and everyone gets into haggling about how much his contribution meant. Instead, Cisco has found that people are eager to become a part of EMTG, without any special compensation. Many of them have been involved in failed start-ups. They are mostly motivated by the desire to see their ideas succeed. More broadly, having a home for ideas such as EMTG, even if those ideas are still not implemented, can serve as something of a pressure valve for a company. It gives people a place to go, someone who will listen, which is useful in its own right.

Cargill's EBA and Cisco's EMTG are exemplars of productive Producer Model organizations. However, the Producer Model is not without its share of challenges and risks. First, it requires significant investments over many years. Large direct costs make such organizations vulnerable to changes in the corporate business climate. Motorola's corporate entrepreneurship group, the Early Stage Accelerator, had an annual budget in the tens of millions of dollars and a dedicated staff of more than 35 people. Despite successfully commercializing dozens of technologies and cutting idea-to-market cycle times in half, it was disbanded when Motorola ran into hard times in 2008.

Also, despite many improvements in how Producer organizations are connected to the corporate strategy and leadership, integrating successful projects into established business units remains an inherent difficulty for a separated organization. Both Cargill and Cisco succeed at this because of the corporate flexibility each has in creating new business units and, more important, the direct interest and engagement of top executives. There is not much that some companies can do to change how they are organized or how they function. BP could not suddenly change the fundamental organization of the oil and gas industry. DuPont's corporate offices could not start doing end runs around the firm's business units. Clearly, this is one of the reasons that BP and DuPont opted for Advocate organizations instead of Producers.

The direct engagement of top executives is an essential element of moving new businesses into full-scale implementation. This is true for all four models of corporate entrepreneurship, but it is a particular requirement for Producer organizations. Without it, project teams may become isolated, and they can be undermined by existing business units, particularly if they are perceived as pilfering top creative talent.

Over time, building credibility and trust throughout the company is critical if the Producer Model is to succeed. Most of the corporate entrepreneurship leaders in our study said that they spend more than half their time on communications within the company, and we have found that successful Producer Model organizations are generally run by senior leaders who have mastered the art of internal corporate politics. This quality makes Producer organizations vulnerable to poor succession planning. (The problem of the leadership of corporate entrepreneurship organizations will be covered in Chapter 5.)

The four models of corporate entrepreneurship are the basic archetypes from which companies can choose. In the next chapter, we will provide guidance as to how to make that choice, based on your organization's strategic intent and corporate context. Before that, however, it is important to emphasize, as the examples in this section have shown, that there is significant variability and customization involved in implementing any one of the models. Furthermore, very large companies may implement different models at different levels of the corporation, or sometimes within the same organization. IBM, for instance, maintains a Producer team called Emerging Business Opportunities that, as mentioned in the introduction, is generating over $15 billion per year in new revenues. Meanwhile, IBM's Thinkplace and Innovation Jams encourage new ideas and networking in the fashion of an Advocate Model. Like an Enabler, IBM supports divisional processes for concept development and experimentation, some of which transfer projects to the Emerging Business Opportunities program for full-scale development and scaling. And IBM is fortunate to have a corporate culture that in many ways supports an Opportunist Model. Distributed power bases enable corporate entrepreneurs to find pockets of interest and resources across the corporation without structured facilitation.

Summary

Chapter 3 cut through the maze of emerging innovation management practices to present four basic corporate entrepreneurship models that a company can adopt. The four models represent archetypal approaches to corporate entrepreneurship.

- *Opportunist Model.* For those organizations with a history and culture that are broadly supportive of internal new business development, corporate entrepreneurship may thrive without any formal office or dedicated funding. All companies, by definition, start as Opportunists; very few succeed exclusively with this model in the long run.
- *Enabler Model.* Some companies retain the open, serendipitous spirit of the Opportunist Model, but designate funding and other support for corporate entrepreneurship, aimed at facilitating individuals and self-formed internal teams across the company.
- *Advocate Model.* In this relatively new type of corporate entrepreneurship, a central office spearheads and orchestrates, driving concept development and the formation of new business teams, but it must persuade business units to provide most of the funding. This method is unlikely to generate concepts that disrupt an existing business, but on occasion it can be transformative.
- *Producer Model.* Finally, in several companies, corporate entrepreneurship is focused in a single, corporatewide, corporate-funded effort. This is typically the model of choice in industries where complex systems must be integrated, such as high-tech and aerospace. Unlike the separate organizations of the past, these groups are full-service organizations, covering the whole corporate entrepreneurship cycle from concept development to initial launch.

Multidivisional companies in which units have significant autonomy may implement different models at different levels of the corporation, reflecting local strategic intent and context. Top Producer organizations typically incorporate insights and wisdom from the Advocate model in terms of recognizing the importance of engagement with people throughout the company.

CHAPTER 4

WHICH MODEL OF CORPORATE ENTREPRENEURSHIP IS RIGHT FOR YOU?

In theory, there is no difference between theory and practice. But in practice, there is.

—LAWRENCE "YOGI" BERRA,
AMERICAN BASEBALL LEGEND

How can you find solutions when you don't even know the questions?

—PROFESSOR DONALD N. FREY, AMERICAN BUSINESS
LEADER, ENGINEER, AND EDUCATOR

Corporate Entrepreneurship and Strategy

As the Romans used to say, "If you don't know where you are going, all roads lead there." It is also true that many corporate entrepreneurship initiatives end up on roads to anywhere, and thus nowhere, at least partly because of a lack of focus and clarity. Many corporate entrepreneurship organizations try to accomplish too much. When senior management allocates funds and assigns the authority for making corporate entrepreneurship happen, the newly anointed corporate entrepreneurship team acquires a mission that is related in some way to generating new paths to growth or enhancing the company's overall innovation effectiveness.

Senior leadership should be lauded for recognizing the importance of innovation and corporate entrepreneurship for the company's long-term health. Unfortunately, without more specific direction, the objectives of corporate entrepreneurship teams often become unwieldy and unclear. When they have unclear objectives, teams tend to overextend their troops, waging too many simultaneous battles. Others in the company, some of whom must become the innovators' allies, end up being unsure of exactly what this cost center is trying to accomplish.

For a corporate entrepreneurship effort to succeed, it must be focused on important and relatively stable corporate objectives. It is not enough to simply set a goal for revenue growth or margin contribution attributable to corporate entrepreneurship. Setting an "innovation aspiration" is important, as it solidifies which bottom-line effects are needed and provides guidance to those who are charged with developing specific structures and processes. It can be a motivating metric that helps the company determine how it will eventually allocate corporate entrepreneurship funding between incremental and breakthrough projects. But that is not enough on its own.

In fact, corporate objectives must be clearly defined so that different parts of the corporation understand their role in the process and can pull together the people, resources, and tools necessary to accomplish these objectives. As you might imagine, there can be considerable negotiation over corporate entrepreneurship roles and missions, particularly the boundaries between corporate entrepreneurship and the existing new product development functions and new business development organizations. There may also be significant pushback from legal or compliance organizations. In making a change as significant as pursuing corporate entrepreneurship, such internal political battles are inevitable.

So how do you engage in successful corporate entrepreneurship? It's a multistage process. At the highest level, the mandate for growth or transformation should be accompanied by a vision that points the general direction. In the case of DuPont, discussed in Chapter 3, CEO Chad Holliday wanted to make a push for better top-line revenue growth, in addition to the cost cutting that had sustained margins and returns for the prior six years. His corporate planning group considered DuPont's strengths, its changing competitive context, and state-of-the-art academic research to articulate a strategic vision. That vision, captured by the phrase "beyond the molecule," described how DuPont could increase top-line growth by adding services and knowledge value to its traditional bulk chemicals business. This charge guided what became Knowledge Intensive University, through which DuPont's most senior leaders were informed of the new growth direction. Knowledge Intensive University provided training and support to DuPont business units that considered this new growth direction to be a valuable and useful way to grow their businesses in support of the CEO's initiative. (Note: Holliday did not mandate that business units must work with the Knowledge Intensive Management team.) Over time, Knowledge Intensive University evolved into the Market-Driven Innovation process, which aimed to bring greater market awareness and focus to emerging business opportunities. Market-Driven Innovation processes have gained wide acceptance across DuPont's business units, its geographical service divisions, and even central research and development.

BP Plc, the global oil giant, is another example of how a top-level mandate combined with a strategic vision can guide decisions about corporate entrepreneurship structures and processes. As discussed in Chapter 3, in the late 1990s, BP's CEO, Lord Browne, was a leader in mega-mergers and acquisitions within the oil industry. In the face of low oil prices and diminishing proven reserves, driving overhead efficiencies and broadening the customer base was the industry's general strategy for driving profit growth. Beyond this, however, Lord Browne believed that there could be "intellectual economies of scale" across the much broader size and scope of BP's businesses. In particular, he believed that information technologies should be seen "not just as a service function but as an activity which could change the nature of the business itself." This was the context in which he asked Daru Darukhanavala in the office of the chief information officer to build an organization for conceiving and pursuing IT-based innovation across BP business units.

As described in Chapter 3, Daru built an advocacy organization focused on bringing external capabilities to bear on BP's business units' most pressing problems. The organization was structured and managed to drive business transformation across BP, consistent with BP's corporate culture. What BP's executive leadership wanted to accomplish, combined with the political realities of implementation, led to the unique organization and processes of the office of the chief technology officer.

High-level visions such as those propagated by DuPont and BP help provide general alignment across the corporation for the direction in which new business development should be pursued. However, in order to make the vision actionable, specific objectives need to be outlined. Is the company seeking corporatewide cultural transformation, or is it looking at the renovation of particular divisions to address either commoditization or disruptive threats? Or perhaps the problem is that people aren't effective in pursuing opportunities that fall between the cracks of the current organization, that is, "whitespace" opportunities.

Consider the following three potential objectives for a corporate entrepreneurship initiative. They encompass the objectives that corporate entrepreneurship teams are typically founded to accomplish.

1. Invent and build truly new businesses for the company.
2. Assist existing business units to create new products or services; in-license or out-license products, technologies, or other intellectual capital to capture value; or transform the way they do business.
3. Nurture a culture of innovation companywide.

Each objective can add value, but each is also quite different from the others. What types of people, capabilities, and processes would your firm require to build new businesses? The emphasis would need to be on market strategy, business model definition, and an entrepreneurial aptitude. You may also benefit from setting up a separate organization to incubate new concepts that don't fit within your existing business units. If you're focused on helping business units apply innovative thinking to established lines of business, having deep technology expertise may or may not be what you need. Many technology-oriented companies gravitate naturally toward new business development through leading new technologies, which requires exceptional engineering and technology expertise. But it may make more sense to focus on licensing existing intellectual property, which requires strong legal, networking, and negotiation skills. More important, bringing unfamiliar ways of thinking to core businesses requires politically savvy individuals with consultative, facilitative, and persuasive capabilities. They probably shouldn't spend much time in a lab, unless it's a lab they're trying to enhance. Instead, they need to spend their time with business units, functional managers, customers, and partners—all of the individuals and organizations that could affect the future success or failure of their business unit "clients" and the corporate entrepreneurship group as a whole. DuPont and BP, for instance, structured their corporate entrepreneurship efforts around this objective.

We've seen newly formed corporate entrepreneurship teams decide to take on more than one of these objectives, and in some cases all three of them. Sometimes teams take on this monumental task with their eyes wide open, while other times the initiatives simply multiply as a result of having creative, eager people on the team or trying to accommodate the interests of multiple top executives. Simultaneously, the team begins to search for new businesses, engage with business unit leaders to revise existing businesses, hunt for new technologies or product concepts, and employ academics and consultants to advocate the value and importance of corporate entrepreneurship to people across the company. These are all noble goals, but trying to accomplish too much at once could put long-term success at risk.

One of the authors worked with a state-funded university technology transfer organization to help diagnose what was going wrong. The answer was simple: the leadership had built a top-flight team of biotechnology experts who were capable of identifying and evaluating biotechnology opportunities. Unfortunately, the team's role was to help the university's researchers commercialize technologies through licensing or new business creation. Bench scientists, with few exceptions, are not the right people to build businesses. Given the legal support it received from the university's lawyers, what the team really needed was entrepreneurial and venture capital skills. Sound obvious? It can be, but we've found that many corporate entrepreneurship teams fail to select people with the necessary skills and tools as a result of insufficient mission focus and clarity.

Let's consider the top-level objectives stated earlier. If a company is seeking to conquer new growth domains, discover breakthrough opportunities, or thwart potentially disruptive competition, then it should consider the Producer Model. In general, business units are unlikely to pursue disruptive concepts and often face strong near-term pressures that discourage investments in new growth platforms. The Producer Model helps overcome this, and it can provide the necessary coordination for initiatives that involve complex technology or require the integration of certain capabilities across different business units.

For companies that want to accelerate the growth of established divisions, the Advocate Model might be the best option. Because of the limited resources of that model, companies must tailor their initiatives to the interests of existing lines of business, and employees have to collaborate intensively throughout the organization. This enhances the potential fit of opportunities with a company's operations, but also requires the leaders to ensure that projects do not become too incremental. Advocates exist to help business units do what they cannot accomplish on their own but should pursue if they are to remain vital and relevant. Moreover, the Advocate Model (as well as the Producer Model) can prevent corporate entrepreneurship from becoming a casualty of powerful business units or competing silos.

Enabler programs can support efforts to enhance a firm's culture, but keep in mind the "culture change traps" highlighted in Chapter 1. When a company *already* enjoys substantial collaboration and ideation at the grassroots level, the Enabler Model can provide clear channels through which concepts can be considered and funded. For companies that are seeking cultural transformation, Enabler processes in combination with new hiring criteria and staff development can result in a number of employees becoming effective change agents. The Enabler Model is particularly well suited to environments in which concept development and experimentation can be pursued economically throughout the organization. At Google, for instance, a Web application prototype might require only a few engineers. In companies with self-managed communities of practice and expert networks, as at many consultancies and technology companies, Enabler programs can accelerate the commercialization of ideas that arise from networks of knowledge workers.

(We will not discuss the Opportunist Model here, since that is the default when none of the deliberate forms of corporate entrepreneurship is selected.)

In all these cases—new platforms, renovation, or transformation—it is important to specify the time frame for change and to consider how specific the objectives should be. Are immediate, bold results required to solve a particular problem, or is the objective an evolutionary program aimed at "blue ocean" discoveries? Crash programs need centralized, strong leadership to move quickly past technical and particularly bureaucratic barriers. Crash programs may even involve multiple parallel efforts, to increase the probability of success. If accomplishing the goal is believed to involve extensions and refinements of known approaches and understanding, then what is wanted is a team of developers and business builders. If a fundamental breakthrough or a highly innovative new approach is required, then scientists and engineers working together with experts in new markets may be needed.

Thinking about Your Corporate Context

Baxter's Path to a Corporate Entrepreneurship Group

The story of Andrea Hunt and Norbert Riedel of Baxter International is an example of how a corporate entrepreneurship effort can emerge from broader thinking about corporate strategy and context. It is illustrative of the kind of progression in thinking seen in several companies that have made corporate entrepreneurship a priority.

Andrea Hunt joined the Chicago area–based medical products company Baxter International in 1988 as part of an internally focused Total Quality Management (TQM) team. At the time, Baxter owned a large distribution business that provided many disposable medical products (gauze, bed linens, tubing, and so on) to hospitals and other health-care providers around the country. After Baxter implemented TQM internally across its own divisions and realized that it could apply its TQM capabilities to the challenges of its suppliers, Hunt's team went from an internal focus to an external focus, providing TQM consulting services. This exposed her to the challenges of product suppliers, integrated delivery networks, and big hospital systems.

By 1992, the TQM consultancy had become a business-as-usual initiative, and Hunt was ready for something new. Baxter's CEO, Dave Auld, was thinking about how Baxter could do a better job of customer satisfaction beyond just the issue of quality. Internally, Baxter faced long-standing employee satisfaction issues that Auld wanted to address. Hunt joined a team that was focused on helping Baxter enhance the underlying values that affect behaviors and performance. The group studied initiatives at leading companies as well as emerging thought leadership. These investigations led to the Baxter Shared Values Initiative: What are the values that are most important to us as a company, and what do we stand for?

The Shared Values Initiative thrust Hunt into active collaboration—and conflict—with many established processes and power bases. But the initiative ultimately helped Baxter quantifiably enhance customer and employee satisfaction through three related efforts: respect for employees, responsiveness to customers, and results for shareholders. Through these broad initiatives, Hunt developed a heightened appreciation for what it takes to do new things within an established company. She began with an extensive training effort, centered on operational managers rather than on Human Resources. (Indeed, Human Resources had to follow, changing its performance evaluations to include accountability for the core values and modifying hiring criteria.)

Importantly, the CEO and his staff were the first to implement these new procedures. This involvement at the highest levels both demonstrated how seriously Baxter took these initiatives and provided critical protection for Hunt. "It's hard enough to create something new, but the tougher hurdle is enabling the new thing to take hold," Hunt told us. "You have to have perseverance and protection to get something like this through." At the same time, she recognized that doing new things was her forte and her passion.

After five years building the "respect" element of the strategy—focusing on teamwork and empowerment—Hunt turned her attention to the "responsiveness" component, which was focused on the customer. Hunt and her team worked with Gallup to explore and understand issues such as customer loyalty. She delved into customer-focused innovation processes. It became increasingly clear to her over time that respect, responsiveness, and results could facilitate a more broadly innovative culture at Baxter.

Thus, the ground was well prepared when, in 1999, the new CEO, Harry Kraemer, made discovering meaningful new growth for the company a strategic priority. Having overcome some earlier operational challenges through the initiatives that Hunt had spearheaded, Baxter decided to address long-term growth and gear up the stock price. Innovation would be critical to success. Kraemer's analysis suggested that there were particular opportunities in the "white spaces" between business units.

To begin, Baxter founded a corporate innovation team (CIT) to address this challenge from a companywide, strategic perspective. The CIT evaluated the project pipeline and identified and filled near-term capability gaps, such as project management. For concepts that required more development but that transcended or cut across Baxter's divisions—areas where existing business units would be unlikely to venture on their own, but where Baxter could still add value—Hunt proposed that Baxter also create an incubator. In 2000, Baxter created a Non-Traditional Research and Innovation (NTRI) group to serve as the incubator. It also formed an innovation leadership team, including six top Baxter corporate executives and the presidents of each of Baxter's divisions, to support the effort. Hunt was chosen to lead the incubator and was named vice president of nontraditional innovation.

Hunt began building Baxter's new business incubator, bringing together people with complementary business skills and significant internal networks. Her team began in 2000 with five core people who possessed "entrepreneurial DNA" and a $3 million budget, and it grew to nearly 15 people and $7 million by early 2002 (out of about a $400 million overall R&D effort). These people, in turn, were building cross-functional teams with people from across Baxter divisions and functions to pursue projects with serious growth potential that would be unlikely to happen within individual business units. The NTRI team would take a concept up to the point where either a traditional R&D organization would adopt it or it was spun out as part of a joint development venture. An NTRI Review Board was formed, with business development, R&D, marketing, or strategy people from each division, as well as some key corporate stakeholders, such as the CFO.

Around the same time as the Non-Traditional Research and Innovation group began its operations, Baxter formed a core technical competencies team to identify and monitor strategically important technology areas, out of which Baxter could create high-margin new products. In 2002, Kraemer named senior Baxter R&D executive Norbert Riedel as corporate chief scientific officer (CSO) with the charge of overseeing these efforts and NTRI at the top executive level.

Soon after her appointment, Hunt discussed the challenge of her new position. "We know innovation outside our business units is critical, but will we have the courage to commit over the long term, especially if the economy becomes a challenge?" Her fear was prescient. The creation of top-level oversight and attention from senior executives was critical in 2004 when, just as the incubator hit its stride, Baxter's performance tumbled and budgets were slashed, putting the incubator's future at risk. If it hadn't been for Hunt's extensive networks throughout the company, not to mention the CEO's and CSO's commitment to the team and its mission, NTRI would have become a casualty. After Baxter CEO Henry Kraemer left the company in 2004, Riedel remained the senior executive sponsor who kept NTRI alive.

Corporate Context, Abstracted

The Baxter case illustrates the organic process of developing a corporate entrepreneurship competency, combining internal business improvement efforts with external demands for growth and a firm leadership imprimatur. In this section, we take a step back and discuss the types of factors beyond strategy and objectives that generally make a difference in selecting a corporate entrepreneurship direction, to guide you in thinking about your own corporate context.

In the early stages of our research—before we focused on the fundamental issues of organizational and resource uncertainties that underlie the four models described in Chapter 3— we asked firms about numerous contextual factors that affected their corporate entrepreneurship efforts. The most often mentioned elements shaping innovation in these companies were constraints and gaps derived from factors internal to the company and external influences in their core markets. The following list covers those elements that were mentioned most often, divided into two categories, which will be broken down and explained in greater detail over the course of the next few pages.

CONTEXT INFLUENCES CORPORATE ENTREPRENEURSHIP

Internal Structure and Culture
- Divisional or business unit autonomy
- Divisional or business unit diversity
- Corporate culture and history with collaboration and entrepreneurship

External Business Environment
- Level of turbulence in the firm's core markets
- Breadth or intensity of technologies underlying offerings
- Capital requirements for commercialization of new business models
- Regulatory restrictions on commercialization of new business models

These factors make a difference in the type of corporate entrepreneurship structure and practices that are most appropriate for your company. For instance, the highly structured and expensive commercialization process for a medical device or pharmaceutical argues for a different type of corporate entrepreneurship design from that used for consumer packaged goods or a new Web site.

Divisional or Business Unit Autonomy

If divisions or business units enjoy a great deal of autonomy in your corporation, a central organization aimed at overcoming the barriers between them—sometimes called silos or stovepipes (or, in the tongue-in-cheek version of one of our clients, "cylinders of excellence")—may be warranted. That central organization might or might not have its own project funding, depending on corporate objectives and processes, as we discussed earlier. In the Baxter case, the corporate entrepreneurship effort followed a series of other centrally driven strategic initiatives, but it was modestly staffed and funded because the creation of executive-level oversight mechanisms provided a ready means for allocating additional funds to promising projects. (We will describe one such project in Chapter 5 when we discuss the leadership of corporate entrepreneurship efforts.)

Divisional or Business Unit Diversity

If business units are in diverse, largely nonoverlapping business areas, then there may be little perceived value in a corporatewide effort. Still, an Advocate-style organization could be seen as a useful way to facilitate local innovation or drive potentially transformative external technologies into business units. If business units are diverse, but there is perceived value in coordinated efforts to build broad solutions, then a central organization dedicated to filling in these so-called white spaces may be valuable. This latter objective was part of the Baxter CEO's vision, hence the creation of the centralized corporate innovation team and Non-Traditional Research and Innovation (NTRI) group at Baxter.

Corporate Culture and History

A company that is considering a corporate entrepreneurship effort but that does not have much of a history or culture of supporting innovative thinking is likely to need a formal corporate effort to overcome corporate inertia and drive new business conceptualization and development. However, a company teeming with entrepreneurial people may find that instituting some Enabler processes is sufficient to make corporate entrepreneurship thrive. In the Baxter case, the creation of a corporate entrepreneurship team followed separate efforts to build a more innovative culture, but pursuing new business creation just through Enabler-style processes was not sufficient. Baxter's NTRI team evolved into a dedicated Producer organization that creates entirely new growth platforms for the company.

Market Turbulence

A company whose core markets are turbulent will probably need to experiment in many different directions in order to find promising new business models. Dedicated resources can help by facilitating fast decision making and action. A decentralized approach in the early stages can help bring in ideas from all areas of the company. For Baxter, whose markets were relatively stable, a decentralized approach could have been adopted if the corporate objective had been to revitalize business units, as opposed to discovering and exploiting white-space opportunities. In fact, business unit innovation became the responsibility of the CSO and the core technical competencies team.

Technical Intensity and Breadth

Companies in technologically intensive markets generally require a centralized corporate entrepreneurship effort in order to build coherent systems. They also may benefit from supporting corporatewide communities of practice to help their people maintain world-class knowledge and skills. In the case of Baxter, it built corporatewide structures and processes—most notably the creation of the executive position of chief science officer—to coordinate its research and development community and to allocate the necessary resources to corporate entrepreneurship efforts.

Capital Requirements

In some markets, large capital expenditures are required in order to commercialize concepts. Such expenditures inevitably involve top-level allocation of resources and an organization that is accountable. For Baxter, which is in the health-care industry, complex commercialization processes were quite familiar, and top-level resource allocation for expensive clinical trials was overseen by top executives.

Regulatory Environment

In highly regulated markets, centralized coordination is essential to ensure compliance. In cases where the regulatory process is also time-consuming and expensive, dedicated, consistent funding for projects is also essential, although it can come from business unit funds rather than corporate-level funds. In the case of Baxter, funding for early project conceptualization and development was centralized, but business units were responsible for regulatory compliance, which arises in later stages.

In sum, an Enabler Model is called for when business units are weak relative to the corporate core, with potential entrepreneurial business builders lacking sufficient support or executive champions inside their business units. An Advocate Model can be best when business units are strong and have growth opportunities that are relatively close to their core or for white-space opportunities when there is relatively poor interaction and coordination across business units. The Producer Model is usually employed when business units are strong, to overcome silos, or when there is turbulence or high entry barriers in existing or targeting markets, requiring a tightly coordinated and consistently resourced approach.

Getting Started: Commitment, Socialization, and Resources

Commitment, socialization, and resources are the first concrete actions toward building a corporate entrepreneurship capability. However, in reality, top-level commitment to goals is a critical aspect of the context in which a corporate entrepreneurship effort operates and therefore must be considered in its design. A corporate entrepreneurship effort that is given close top executive attention, backed up by prompt and decisive action, may be freer to experiment with riskier approaches than one that enjoys less direct or intensive top executive support. A corporate entrepreneurship effort that enjoys a strong imprimatur from the CEO will have an easier time bringing in top people, both internally and externally, building out and applying sophisticated management tools, and undertaking expensive demonstrations. Absent such consistent and visible CEO support, a corporate entrepreneurship effort may need to be designed more conservatively.

Corporate entrepreneurship efforts are almost always vulnerable to successions in leadership and changes in the prospects of the core business. And executive commitment alone cannot make things happen. Leadership will not improve the prospects for corporate entrepreneurship success if sufficient effort has not been undertaken to characterize, understand, and address knowledge gaps or to manage expectations. The problem of moving forward with corporate entrepreneurship in the face of less-than-vigorous (or misguided) top executive support is discussed in Chapter 5.

In general, we have observed that companies that are considering a corporate entrepreneurship endeavor generally undertake the following steps, which we will discuss in turn.

- *Point the way.* Articulate a strategic vision for growth that is consistent with the core capabilities that corporate entrepreneurship can leverage.
- *Delineate objectives.* Start with a small team to clearly define and communicate the company's objectives for corporate entrepreneurship.
- *Neutralize the naysayers.* Build corporate and divisional leadership consensus through extensive communication.
- *Select and support a corporate entrepreneurship model.* Companies need to select the right model (Enabler, Advocate, or Producer), develop a team with the required capabilities, and provide the necessary resources.
- *Start with quick wins.* It's important to build credibility with tangible performance early on and to learn lessons to protect programs from marginalization or cancellation.

- *Evolve.* Objectives and contexts change over time, and so must programs for corporate entrepreneurship. Expectations need to be continuously explained and managed.

Point the Way

We started this chapter by discussing the problem of articulating a strategic vision for growth, as this is a critical—yet often insufficiently considered—starting place for launching a corporate entrepreneurship effort. The key question is this: What should we be pursuing, given what we know and our level of commitment, and in what time frame? If this question is answered too narrowly, the company will get more of the same. If it is answered too broadly, people won't know where to start. When everyone knows what they're looking for, they're more likely to find it.

The Innovation Radar, described in Chapter 2, provides one way to articulate strategic direction. Successful companies tend to focus on two to four key dimensions, based on corporate strategy, and to build broad competency in them—including flexibility and continuous learning—as a competitive advantage. Corporate leadership may undertake strategic planning efforts to identify which dimensions of corporate entrepreneurship look most promising for creating competitive advantage, then provide these to the person or team formulating the corporate entrepreneurship approach. For example, P&G's "connect and develop" approach leverages its strength and resilience in value capture, customer knowledge, presence, and brand. Apple Computer's exquisite design of complete customer solutions—not just the product designs for which it is famous—combined with its branding and networking prowess is the key to its success in corporate entrepreneurship. Google innovates by facilitating entrepreneurially minded employees in devising novel business systems that leverage the firm's powerful search and advertising platforms.

Again, companies should not try to innovate over all elements of the business system at once. If it seems that every aspect of the business system needs to change for a corporate entrepreneurship effort to be successful, then the company should consider a different approach, such as corporate venture investing.

Delineate Objectives

The issue of objectives was also covered at the beginning of the chapter, since this is an equally critical executive decision preceding the disciplined pursuit of corporate entrepreneurship. Is the objective to build radical new growth platforms or to renovate existing business units? Is cultural transformation part of the equation, or is the goal to unleash latent entrepreneurial talent?

Deciding among these objectives can take a considerable amount of time and socialization. The first step, in general, is to nominate a leader for the effort, or to pull together a small, credible team to investigate and propose how to proceed with corporate entrepreneurship. This person or team will face resistance, guaranteed. Some pushback may come from business units that are fearful of loss of turf. Some may come from corporate functions such as research and development or business development, which might perceive corporate entrepreneurship as being under their purview. But over time, and with a combination of skill and top executive pressure, a consensus (or at least acquiescence) is likely to emerge among senior management regarding objectives and a path forward.

Neutralize the Naysayers

Although it may be possible to achieve support from most business units and other corporate leaders, there will always be latent resistance, particularly as the group starts to come into being and begins calling on corporate resources such as marketing or production for support. Continuing communication is essential, not only to build support for the new initiative, but also to prevent internal stakeholders from regarding corporate entrepreneurship as a drain on or threat to the company's established businesses. New leaders of corporate entrepreneurship initiatives are often surprised by how much time they spend talking with corporate and business unit management, beyond the initial discussion when the effort was first being formulated. As we stated at the beginning of the chapter, people—particularly those who need to be your allies—are going to wonder what exactly this cost center is trying to accomplish. In some companies, they may passively work to derail the fledgling effort.

To some extent, such resistance can be limited by simply telling people what you are doing and keeping them in the loop consistently. In addition, an early set of "quick wins" creates credibility. The bottom line is that building new businesses requires contributions from people across the firm, especially during launch and scaling, so communication remains critical even after a corporate entrepreneurship program has established a proven track record.

Select and Support a Corporate Entrepreneurship Model

After consideration of strategic objectives and contextual factors, and after extensive socialization, the right structure for your corporate entrepreneurship effort will probably be quite clear. Once a structure is selected, it is critical that the appropriate resources be applied. (Again, the Opportunist Model is the default when no choice is made.)

With respect to resources, the Enabler Model can generally be maintained in a much leaner fashion than either the Advocate or the Producer Model. Simple processes for project selection, communicated firmwide and arbitrated by a senior team, and with limited staff (sometimes just a single person), can suffice. If your company is fortunate enough to have lots of entrepreneurial staff and a culture that supports risk taking, then relatively few additional resources need to be devoted to corporate entrepreneurship. The key support required for the Enabler Model is well-defined senior executive attention, so that promising concepts can be moved forward expeditiously. Well-designed and executed Enabler processes have the added benefit of exposing top executives to rising talent in the company, so that they can be moved into high-growth, strategic areas of the business.

Implementing an Advocate Model, which focuses on bringing innovative thinking to established lines of business, does not require a large budget. What is essential for an Advocate Model to work, as mentioned earlier in the chapter, is to have individuals with the instincts and access to navigate your corporate culture and facilitate change. However, some funding is required to develop and implement methodologies, create new business design tools, and, most important, build and maintain internal and external networks.

As companies increasingly look outside for technologies and business development partners, the networking element of corporate entrepreneurship is being recognized as a new kind of competency, one that can benefit from explicit, dedicated management. Active network development can greatly facilitate concept development; absent such a network, significant time and energy will be required to identify and mobilize expertise for each new concept. Venture capital firms employ full-time people to identify external resources that are capable of adding value to new ventures and investment selection.

For instance, some companies have for many years supported communities of practice or expert communities to cross-fertilize specialized knowledge across the company. To apply a market metaphor, communities of practice generate liquidity for knowledge markets. Innovative concepts can be generated anywhere within an organization. Unfortunately, they are often created in locations where they are unlikely to be acted upon. An effective community of practice helps move concepts to the right location for action.

Recently, information technology has enabled broader and deeper opportunities for such organizations through online blogs and wikis. The Internet age has also fostered a new type of episodic but structured knowledge networking: the online R&D marketplace. Firms such as InnoCentive, NineSigma, and yet2.com seek to bring clients with scientific or technical problems together with scientists worldwide who might have solutions to those problems. Such forums have accelerated the discovery and formation of connections among disparate disciplines and industries, which are so often the source of innovation.

More aggressive still, some companies that are committed to corporate entrepreneurship have designated specific individuals to pursue networking. These network builders are to be "door openers" for technical evaluators, as well as people who can attract top talent to participate on corporate entrepreneurship teams. Research by Richard Leifer and his colleagues in the 2000 book *Radical Innovation* suggests that two types of networking support personnel are particularly beneficial: (1) "hunters," who actively seek out ideas with application potential, and (2) "gatherers," who understand strategic needs and are poised to recognize and technically validate promising new ideas. "Hunters have technical training, but they are more likely to be experienced in marketing or business development" (in an industrial environment) or in high-level systems management (in government). "Perhaps as important, a successful hunter knows how to articulate the opportunity in compelling terms that gain the attention of higher management—something that few bench scientists are skilled at doing." Gatherers, on the other hand, "have the technical sophistication to assess what they encounter. In addition, their life experiences have engendered a certain . . . awareness of markets and social and scientific trends. . . . First-line and midlevel research managers and senior scientists [often play] the role of gatherer."

People with the disposition and orientation to be hunters or gatherers can be hard to find. Recall from the BP example in Chapter 3 that Darukhanavala would spend as long as a full year to make a single hire, since effective networking with the IT community was essential to the corporate entrepreneurship model of his group. For those he hired externally, he knew that he could teach them what they needed to learn about the oil industry, but he could not teach them how to be effective innovation networkers.

Finally, implementing a Producer Model organization clearly requires serious capital and staffing and typically a direct line to top management. Understaffed, part-time, or underfunded Producer teams are set up for failure. Clearly, the dedicated team and capital required by the Producer Model make it the most resource-intensive choice. As discussed earlier, the kind of people needed for such an organization are those with an entrepreneurial aptitude, strong knowledge in market strategy and business model definition, and skills in networking. As with an Advocate organization, the leader of such an effort needs to be politically savvy and respected within the corporation, so that homes can be found for successfully incubated concepts. Separated organizations face the hardest battle in reintegrating new businesses back into the corporate core. We'll discuss this problem a bit more in the following section, on transition and scaling challenges.

Keep in mind, also as pointed out in Chapter 3, that very large companies may implement different models at different levels of the corporation, or sometimes even within the same organization. We explained how IBM maintains a Producer team called Emerging Business Opportunities, while ThinkPlace and Innovation Jams encourage ideation and networking in the fashion of an Advocate Model. Like an Enabler, IBM supports divisional processes for concept development and experimentation, and IBM has distributed power bases that enable corporate entrepreneurs to opportunistically find pockets of interest and resources across the corporation without structured facilitation.

Start with Quick Wins

The early stages of building a corporate entrepreneurship team should be dynamic and exploratory; however, the trial-and-error approach must be balanced by the recognition that the corporation has a limited horizon for seeing a return on its investment. Make sure that when the reviews come around, you can show some early successes, while protecting the longer-term game changers. Teams that seek only game changers often fail to win the right and the runway to see them take flight.

Whatever corporate entrepreneurship model you're pursuing, it's a good idea to focus initially on a small number of projects that can be brought to successful fruition quickly, that is, the "low-hanging fruit." Early success builds credibility, and it makes communicating the corporate entrepreneurship group's mission easier. (At one company we know, the corporate entrepreneur-ship team made efforts to garner local press coverage, which it discovered was superior to internal memos as a method of getting the word out.) More important, the corporate entrepreneurship group needs to be ready to show tangible performance when the CFO's office calls and asks, "What are we getting for our money?" Be ready to answer that question at a moment's notice, because chances are you'll have to.

Recall from the BP case in Chapter 3 that many executives were initially skeptical about the role and potential impact of a small group like the CTO office. As business successes mounted, skepticism gave way to support, and the office's brand and impact grew. Based on its reputation for solving problems (without becoming too caught up in bureaucratic processes), it began receiving unprompted questions from business unit managers. It increasingly came to be perceived as a strategic contributor to BP business units.

Evolve

Another advantage of starting with quick wins is that such experiences also generate early lessons about what works and what does not. Whatever initial organization your company creates to pursue corporate entrepreneurship, it should be designed knowing that it is going to change. Successful corporate entrepreneurship requires adaptation in order to generate self-sustaining new businesses on a consistent basis. Expectations across the company need to be continuously explained and managed.

The BP case from Chapter 3 is an excellent example. The office of the CTO began with broad networking events with an external focus—finding promising IT technologies and suppliers—but over time it evolved toward an operating motif that was increasingly driven by its business unit partnerships. At the same time, Darukhanavala's team at BP was so successful that senior management applied pressure to his group to expand. The group resisted, arguing that it was precisely its focus and dynamic team approach that made it successful. Instead, the group found new ways to add value without expanding the core team or changing the mission. Business unit partnering was a way to increase its value to the corporation without abandoning the basic strategic model.

In the final section, we'll consider some of the "down the road" issues that may influence your corporate entrepreneurship design. Before doing so, Table 4-1 summarizes the points made in this chapter about the three deliberate models of corporate entrepreneurship.

Down the Road: The Transition and Scaling Challenge

When you begin your corporate entrepreneurship effort in earnest, you will naturally begin by collecting ideas and performing initial screening and due diligence to find the most promising concepts. Many companies have made the formerly "fuzzy front end" of the corporate entrepreneurship process more systematic and productive by implementing explicit procedures for generating, collecting, and evaluating new business ideas, for example, scenario planning, technology scouting, disciplined IP management, stage-gate milestone management, and portfolio risk management tools. Your corporate entrepreneurship effort may involve setting up an incubator to shepherd promising new business concepts.

However, despite these sound planning and management efforts, corporate entrepreneurship projects often stall at the

Table 4-1

	Enabler Model	Advocate Model	Producer Model
Strategic Goal	Facilitate entrepreneurial employees and teams	Reinvigorate or transform business units; support corporate entrepreneurship teams	Exploit crosscutting or disruptive opportunities
Essential Function	Provide independent funding and top executive attention to future business leaders with new ideas	Evangelize, coach, and facilitate business units in pursuing new opportunities	Provide full-service corporate entrepreneurship by conceiving, screening, funding, coaching, scaling, and reintegrating new business concepts
Inputs	Dedicated money, executive engagement, and recruiting and personnel development	Well-connected corporate veterans with a small staff of business-building coaches and a CEO imprimatur	Well-connected corporate veteran leadership with full-time staff and significant, independent funding
Outputs	Proven concepts, but generally within the firm's strategic frame (Note: Enabler programs can also help facilitate overall cultural change.)	New businesses relatively close to a business unit core or significant business unit process efficiencies	Self-sustaining and/or potentially disruptive new businesses that may or may not fit any existing business unit

Success Factors	• Culture of innovation • Structural flexibility for teams to pursue projects • Well-defined executive involvement in milestone funding decisions • Effectively communicated selection process and criteria	• Expertise in building new businesses • Significant team facilitation capabilities • Skill in coalition building and internal and external networking • C-level visibility and support	• Expertise in building new businesses • Respected leadership with significant internal decision authority • Explicit attention to corporate entrepreneurship executive career incentives
Typical Challenges	• Senior executive bandwidth • Maintaining coherence and discipline with respect to corporate brands • Finding and satisfying project champions (that is, making sure Enabler processes do not become a "black hole" for ideas)	• Overcoming business unit near-term pressures • Finding "business builders" among executives traditionally rewarded more for execution than for innovation	• Reintegrating successful projects into the core • Leadership succession • Lack of business unit support

"back end," that is, at the point of scaling field-proven new business concepts and making the transition into self-sustaining businesses. In other words, the corporate entrepreneurship bottleneck today is no longer coming up with ideas or developing new concepts, but rather scaling in the marketplace and finding an organizational home for the business within the company.

Today's transition and scaling challenges can be traced back to the changes in R&D management practices discussed briefly in Chapter 1, where heavy investments in laboratories gave way to research networks because of problems in commercializing the outputs of separated laboratories. (See Appendix B for a fuller history of corporate entrepreneurship.) Some of the problems are fundamental: in many companies, corporate entrepreneurship projects outgrow their incubators but don't produce sufficient revenues to garner the attention of business units preoccupied with meeting this quarter's numbers. Some of the problems are firm-specific: in one company we've studied, profitable new businesses run into trouble when the business units receiving them impose their particular quality and product development standards retroactively.

Because transition and scaling has only recently been identified as a specific issue, it's useful to briefly review recent writings. As is often the case in a newly emerging literature, each author offered a different framework. Nevertheless, certain management principles for transition and scaling success may be gleaned.

- Geoffrey Moore's landmark 1991 book *Crossing the Chasm* pointed out that technology companies often fail because they do not understand that mainstream customers, unlike early adopters, will require significant support if they are to adopt an offering that requires users to change their behavior patterns in order to fully benefit from it. Moore advises firms to focus on customer segments for whom the bottom-line benefits of a new way of doing business are compelling, then work intensely with these customers to make sure they are satisfied. Doing so leads these customers to become references for other risk-averse managers in adjacent industries. As the Allied powers did on D-Day, firms need to focus their energies on securing a small beachhead in the mainstream market and then branching out from there.

- Clayton Christensen's 1997 book, *The Innovator's Dilemma*, noted that established firms are often upended by competitors that offer products that have lower performance but are simpler, more convenient, or less expensive. Initially, low-end customers who are "overserved" by the market leaders adopt these products. But often the new technical approach advances to intersect the needs of mainstream customers. Christensen terms these "disruptive innovations" because they undermine the competencies and incentives perfected by the established firm, which is ill equipped to recognize and adjust to the threat to its core business. To rectify this, in his 2003 follow-up book, *The Innovator's Solution*, Christensen suggests that top-level commitment and an independent organization are the keys to adjusting to the threat, particularly to addressing internal resistance to transition and scaling. He also argues that businesses need to find people with the right disposition and experience to cope with the uncertainties of managing the early stages of a new growth business. Christensen notes that firms with larger numbers of relatively autonomous business units have tended to perform better because the growth demands of an individual unit are much smaller than the growth targets of the overall corporation, and hence more opportunities look attractive (and there are more managers looking for such opportunities).

- A joint project by the Industrial Research Institute (IRI) and Rensselaer Polytechnic Institute (RPI) delved into the management competencies required for large, established firms to conceive, refine, and launch a *Radical Innovation* (2000). To overcome the disincentives that business units face in scaling innovative projects and finding appropriate mainstream business models, they suggest that companies form a transition team, assess transition readiness, develop a detailed transition plan, identify transition senior management champions, establish a transition oversight board, provide transition funding and commitment, and define the business model to lay the groundwork for a big market.

- The same types of suggestions appear in David Garvin and Lynne Levesque's overview article in a 2006 *Harvard Business Review*, "Meeting the Challenges of Corporate Entrepreneurship." One-third of the "balancing acts" that firms face concern integrating field-proven new business concepts into the corporate core. They advocate that corporate entrepreneurship projects that are at the point of scaling begin to share operational responsibilities with an existing business, mixing in managers and building "dotted- and solid-line reporting relationships," while formulating specific criteria for fully integrating the new business into the existing business.

- In *Fast Second* (2005), Constantinos Markides and Paul Geroski recommend that large firms focus on scaling up (consolidating) strategically selected segments of emerging markets, rather than investing significant amounts of R&D in trying to create emerging technologies. This should be done just as a shakeout in the industry is close to producing a "dominant design." They also incorporate the insights of Christensen, recommending that large firms apply their product realization advantages over start-ups to produce simpler, more convenient, or less expensive solutions based on the dominant design. Once the mass market has emerged, continuing innovation in business models is required to hold one's position.

Summarizing the literature, there appears to be an emerging consensus on certain aspects of the transition and scaling challenges. The value of a technology or process innovation depends on the business model through which it goes to market, and continuing innovation in business models is required to discover the most compelling value propositions for strategically chosen customer segments. As cited in the introduction, this movement from technology-focused innovation toward business model innovation was captured in the 2006 IBM CEO survey, which found that "companies that have grown their operating margins faster than their competitors were putting twice as much emphasis on business model innovation than underperformers."

But established firms today are generally not good at recognizing and pursuing new business models. Moore's D-Day advice is helpful from the customer perspective but has little to say about internal transitions. Christensen emphasizes the importance of what we would call "business builders" and the benefits of organizational separation. IRI/RPI and Garvin and Levesque focus on planning mechanisms and funding commitments that can help corporate entrepreneurship projects over the scaling hump and into an organizational home. Markides and Geroski make the radical suggestion that firms focus on scouting for external start-ups and develop competencies for applying their existing go-to-market competencies to these fledgling businesses.

These are all good suggestions, but the literature's focus on the type of innovation as the unit of analysis (e.g., radical, disruptive, or discontinuous) can disguise actionable insights for managers. *Scaling up proven new concepts and making the transition to an ongoing business can be difficult for a company, regardless of whether the underlying concept is radical, disruptive, or discontinuous.* We believe that the appropriate unit of analysis for helping firms cope with transition and scaling challenges is not the product or technology in question, but rather the firm's business systems. We noted earlier that a corporate entrepreneurship effort should generally be focused along particular business system dimensions. If the transition and scaling of proven concepts is understood to be a dominant problem, then the corporate entrepreneurship focus may need to emphasize those dimensions of the business system that are most closely associated with transition and scaling: customers, organization, supply chain, and networks.

Beyond this, we've noticed four practices that appear to make transition and scaling a surmountable challenge for firms:

- *Engage in complete business system design up front, to help anticipate where the transition and scaling problems are likely to occur.* A new business system design will typically involve changes in several dimensions of your business system at once. Some firms have formal processes for integrating their basic assumptions about customer value propositions and the competitive ecosystem as they consider different business systems. This type of planning seems to help firms anticipate transition and scaling challenges. Chapter 2 covered some of the elements of complete business system planning.

- *Explicitly address business unit disincentives.* "Corporate antibodies" to new businesses are the bane of corporate entrepreneurship projects. Firms that address the problem head-on tend to do better. One of the more effective methods, as suggested by Christensen, is to simply create a new business unit to house the new opportunity. Some firms have standard processes for creating and staffing new business units. Others have formal, corporate-level processes—for example, control of personnel development—that serve to mediate business unit interests.

  In some companies, bypassing existing business units is not considered workable. In such cases, the suggestions of the IRI/RPI research team, emphasizing explicit transition planning, especially for resources, are sound. In such a context, corporate entrepreneurship projects are generally required to obtain investment and oversight from business units, sometimes at relatively early stages of the process. A company can decide where along the line existing business units must be brought in, depending on the kind of corporate entrepreneurship objectives it has promulgated.

- *Hire and support forward-thinking "business builder" managers who are skilled at navigating the turbulence of transition and scaling.* Many authors have noted that the right manager for a corporate entrepreneurship project is not the same as the right manager for the development of a new product or for an acquisition. Successful corporate entrepreneurship projects demand flexibility in building the business model, which requires a different type of experience and disposition from early-stage exploration or from management of an established business. One advantage of forming a dedicated corporate entrepreneurship organization is that it provides a home for business builders within the firm and a mechanism for giving them visibility with top executives. We'll come back to the importance of business builders in Chapter 5.

• *Build competencies in experimentation during the scaling phase.* For some firms—especially those whose products are complex or highly integrated—the ability to build and experiment with prototypes efficiently is valuable. The famed Lockheed "Skunk Works" is an example of this model. Google Labs is another, which is particularly compelling for its market space, given the ease of building and testing Web-based applications. Building prototypes permits early market experimentation and adaptation, which can be invaluable for finding the most compelling customers and business models through which to go to market. The philosophy here needs to be to "fail early and cheaply" rather than spending too much time and money on elegant, corporate-sanctioned experiments that may be designed more for internal political reasons than for expeditiously advancing concrete learning goals for a concept. Thomas Edison's words should be a guide to expedient experimental design: "I have not failed. I have merely found ten thousand ways that won't work."

Summary

You need a corporate entrepreneurship space that is big enough to achieve your growth objectives, and a firm that is capable of acting in this expanded arena. The first point requires discovering a definition of core and growth areas that is consistent with achieving the firm's strategic objectives. The second point requires addressing constraints and expanding capabilities in strategically selected dimensions of the firm's business system. Leading companies do both well.

The challenge of selecting and implementing a corporate entrepreneurship model involves, first, determining which objectives take priority. This will strongly shape the model of corporate entrepreneurship that you select. Once you are clear about your priorities, other requirements become clearer. Who should be part of the team? What tools should we employ? What internal and external partners should we cultivate? How will we make the transition of proven concepts into an existing or new business unit? Next, identify critical partners around the company and focus on some near-term quick wins. Pay special attention to wins that benefit people in positions of authority, people from around the company who can become partners for your corporate entrepreneurship initiatives. You'll need them to tell your story on your behalf, as well as to help you understand what will add the most value. Sharing success stories across the company can contribute to positive change without engaging the culture change challenge head-on. Corporate entrepreneurship is an intangible concept for many people; witnessing it happen in one's own organization makes it real. Finally, keep an open mind and evolve. Those early projects will hold important lessons for what is likely to work on an ongoing basis, and will prove beneficial in identifying any possible pitfalls.

Once a corporate entrepreneurship effort has begun in earnest, keep in mind that the corporate entrepreneurship bottleneck today typically arises at scaling in the marketplace and finding an organizational home for the new business within the company. That is the point at which significantly more resources will need to be devoted, causing internal opponents to mobilize, and the risk of loss will be higher. To address this challenge, we suggest that you

- Engage in complete business system design up front, to help anticipate where the transition and scaling problems are likely to occur.
- Explicitly address business unit disincentives. (One of the more effective methods, when possible, is to simply create a new business unit to house the new opportunity.)
- Hire and support forward-thinking "business builder" managers who are skilled at navigating the turbulence of transition and scaling.
- Build competencies in experimentation during the scaling phase.

CHAPTER 5

LEADERSHIP FROM ALL LEVELS

There are many elements to a campaign. Leadership is number one. Everything else is number two.
—BERTOLT BRECHT (1898–1956), GERMAN AUTHOR

Anyone can steer the ship when the sea is calm.
—PUBLILIUS SYRUS (FIRST CENTURY BCE),
ROMAN AUTHOR AND POET

The House of the Emperor

Confucius taught that the culture of the empire comes down from the house of the emperor. The same is true for companies. The most important levers for creating and nurturing innovative practices are the actions of the CEO and his or her team. For companies that desire to instill a more innovative culture throughout the company—a daunting, long-term task—the leadership of the CEO is essential. If the CEO's team doesn't exhibit a strong interest in innovative, entrepreneurial activities, then these activities will not happen on a significant, ongoing basis. Lots of innovation can occur at the grass roots, but if it doesn't eventually percolate up and receive the support it requires—or, worse yet, if these actions are actively thwarted—people will stop trying. The most persistent, passionate people will either give up or leave and start a new venture. In this context, Mahatma Gandhi's social change adage, "Be the change you envision," provides excellent advice. People within organizations emulate and play to those who succeed. If you want innovative behavior, then start exhibiting it yourself.

Most meaningful endeavors require leadership. Corporate entrepreneurship requires better-integrated, more focused, and more powerful leadership than most other corporate activities. By definition, a new business upsets the status quo and requires individuals within the corporation to do things differently. Momentum, risk aversion, and a company's existing incentive systems are just a few of the hurdles facing active leadership in its pursuit of corporate entrepreneurship. Although frustrating, many of the obstacles to corporate entrepreneurship exist for understandable, often rational reasons. Elements of sound management such as handling financial risk, keeping business units running smoothly in their core area, and driving efficiency are essential to ongoing business success. But they can also impede the development of new businesses.

Of course, employees should be given incentives to maximize the near-term performance of their business units or functions. Unfortunately, this usually means that new business opportunities, which may take time to conceive and develop, take a backseat to projects aimed at making incremental improvements to larger, existing revenue generators. For example, if a $1 billion business unit has an opportunity to leverage a new venture with current revenues of $1 million, how important can this new venture really be? Barring incentives or other mechanisms to encourage giving attention to the new venture, typical business unit salespeople might prefer to sell another $10 million of what they've got and understand, as opposed to investing the time and effort necessary to sell the first $100,000 of something new and unfamiliar.

For this and for many other reasons, corporate entrepreneurship requires substantial and constant leadership from the CEO on down. The leaders must set the growth agenda and work to build an environment in which corporate entrepreneurship can flourish. This does not mean that the entire company must be transformed to have a culture of innovation. But there must at least be a space for such activities, a space that is under the watchful protection of a senior executive.

Ultimately, any individual in the company may drive or support new ventures. In this chapter, we discuss two groups that have a particular responsibility for helping new businesses succeed: senior executives—including corporate, functional, and business unit leaders—and corporate entrepreneurship program leaders.

The Role of Senior Executives in Corporate Entrepreneurship

Throughout years of study, we have not discovered a single firm in which successful new business creation occurs on a sustained basis without significant support from senior leadership. This does not mean senior executives must devote extensive amounts of time and effort to corporate entrepreneurship. Most senior executives have limited time to focus on new business creation. The wider his or her purview, the less time a leader has to focus on any particular activity. However, it must be clear to everyone that senior executives are engaged and committed to corporate entrepreneurship.

As we have emphasized numerous times in previous chapters, corporate entrepreneurship needs to be a deliberate, strategically driven act. The Conference Board reports that while CEOs believe that 40 to 50 percent of their time should be dedicated to the firm's strategy, most CEOs typically report devoting closer to 10 to 15 percent of their time to that task. The reality is that if senior management desires organic growth through new business creation to be more than just an occasional and against-all-odds occurrence, *they must be personally involved*. Corporate entrepreneurship demands that people change and take risks. Few people will do this aggressively without the imprimatur and backing of leadership to overcome the inevitable resistance of organizations and individuals who will be asked to do things differently.

In any project, there will typically be organizational impediments that corporate entrepreneurs cannot (and should not) be expected to overcome alone. This is where senior management can step in, assume a leadership role, and assist. Some examples are

- Calling functional leaders when their people are not responding to requests for information or assistance
- Running interference with business unit managers who are unsure whether they want the new venture to succeed
- Helping to recruit the talent required to take on the challenges of a new venture when sticking with established operations would be easier

Fortunately, we've observed that senior executives do not necessarily need to spend a lot of time on such activities. If they have been clear, consistent, and forceful in early battles over corporate entrepreneurship, they may develop a reputation for intervention that, ironically, may make it less necessary for them to intervene. Consider the case of former U.S. Secretary of Defense William J. Perry, who shepherded the early development of stealth fighter aircraft in the 1970s, when he was the undersecretary for defense research, the third-ranking official in the U.S. Department of Defense. At the time, the concept was not embraced by the U.S. Air Force, which initially saw little value in a relatively slow plane with limited maneuverability. This type of fighter plane, if it could be built, would only marginally improve the Air Force's performance in its current missions. But Perry understood that the plane could perform missions against highly defended targets that the Air Force would not attempt because of the high loss rates, and that the ability to undertake such missions could transform conventional warfare to the advantage of the United States. This is the type of corporate entrepreneurship project—one that requires new types of organizational behaviors—for which senior leadership steering is essential.

Perry chaired a special executive team overseeing the development program. The program manager would report technical and bureaucratic problems to the team. Perry would handle bureaucratic problems personally. After a few months, he noticed that fewer and fewer bureaucratic problems seemed to be arising. The program manager reported that the reason was Perry's direct, personal involvement at the beginning. Word got around that he would use his authority to break bureaucratic logjams. This knowledge created an imputed authority for the program manager, making Perry's personal intervention less necessary as time went on. We'll return to the stealth case later in the chapter.

We've seen a few exceptions that prove the rule: new business creation that was successful without senior management backing. Against the odds, a team within a large industrial company built a new business that ended up creating an entirely new product category. However, despite the product's exceptional growth and great margins, the parent company ended up spinning off the business, stating that it did not fit within the corporation's long-term strategy. This could have been the right strategic decision, to remain focused on the core, but the new products were clearly relevant for the company. However, the design of the new business just didn't fit neatly within the company's established operating model. Meanwhile, members of the senior team continued to beat the organic growth drum. They expressed pleasure at the generation of the new business, but by the divestiture, they sent the unfortunate message to the company that new, relevant businesses were not where they saw the company going. Thus, even when corporate entrepreneurs succeed without senior management support, which is quite rare, their ventures can be compromised if leadership fails to see the strategic fit within the established company. Where possible, engage top management and keep it engaged.

Internal ventures are inherently different from other aspects of operating a corporation. Most functions, even core functions such as sales, marketing, and operations, are run by hierarchies of people who are competent at accomplishing their tasks. These tasks fit clearly within the company's established business systems. One of the challenges of new business creation, and one of the reasons that it demands senior management's attention, is that by definition, new businesses do not fit neatly within a firm's established "business-as-usual" model.

Both active and passive resistance impede new business creation, creating challenges that require serious attention from senior management. Active constraints include such things as capital allocation conflicts (it's easier to allocate capital to established businesses that are making money), turf wars, and internal concerns over the threat of cannibalization of existing revenues. These constraints generally result in active behaviors hostile to new business success. Passive resistance arises from the lack of priority that existing businesses generally place on new businesses. To some extent, this is both expected and reasonable. Most people should spend most of their time on business-as-usual challenges. The trouble occurs when new businesses fail to receive what they need from others within the company simply because of this prioritization process.

The solution to both active and passive constraints naturally begins with the entrepreneurial team itself, but overcoming these obstacles often requires involvement beyond top management. Corporate entrepreneurs must design their development and launch plans with sensitivity to what the core businesses require. It is unreasonable to ask an ongoing business unit to pay special attention to an opportunity that will not generate enough revenues or profits to help the unit meet its long-term growth targets.

These threats can be partly managed by making clear, strategic bets on emerging businesses in ways that signal to the organization that the new business initiative is central to the future of the company. However, even with a sufficient budget and senior management endorsement, corporate entrepreneurs often find it quite difficult to marshal the attention and resources from across the firm that they need if they are to succeed. Corporate entrepreneurs need attention in various ways and at various times from most of the functions within a firm.

Even in cases where firms construct dedicated, well-functioning cross-functional teams with representatives from all relevant functions, the corporate entrepreneurship team will require attention from various members of line businesses and corporate functions, not to mention external partners. This can engender frustration and even resentment, because the new business typically is not a top priority for people outside of the core team. Everyone in the company already has a clearly defined job, and people may not feel inclined to devote more time and energy to the needs of the leader of a prerevenue business that is not connected to their typical responsibilities.

While rejection is often an active process, new businesses can also sometimes fall victim to benign neglect. Indifferent or well-meaning people may fail to provide assistance when the corporate entrepreneurship team needs it. Only senior management has the resources to overcome both active resistance and benign neglect, and this antirejection effort must persist throughout the development and launch phases of the new business. A new business is never safe until it has proven its financial impact on the firm's top and bottom lines.

In many ways, new business creation within an existing firm is analogous to a human organ transplant. Following an organ transplant, the human immune system quickly recognizes the implanted organ as a foreign object and attempts to isolate or destroy it. Without the ongoing administration of powerful antirejection drugs, the host body will reject the organ, even at the expense of its own survival. Without a proper cultural context, structures, and processes, established, complex corporations will ferret out foreign entities in much the same manner.

Those precious few firms that have been able to foster entrepreneurship across the company, such as the Google and Whirlpool cases we examined earlier, provide the exceptions that prove the rule. Even in these cases, we observe a cultural substrate that is supportive of entrepreneurial activity and a top management consensus regarding new business creation as a focal objective of the firm. Ultimately, only top management can administer the medicine that is necessary to avoid rejection. While proper structures and processes go a long way, maintaining the firm's focus, effecting culture change, and maintaining the right cultural environment for corporate entrepreneurship begin with the CEO's team and remain under its ongoing stewardship.

Even in companies in which entrepreneurial activities have become natural and are ingrained in the structures and processes of the firm, a shift in focus at the top can lead, over time, to entrepreneurial atrophy. For example, 3M has been famous since the 1960s for consistently introducing new businesses built around innovative technology platforms. After 2000, however, under the leadership of former GE executive James McNerney, 3M appeared to lose some of its creative luster, Brian Hindo suggested in a 2007 *BusinessWeek* article. McNerney emphasized performance reviews based on Six Sigma quality control principles, which focus on efficiency. But in 2005, when McNerney left 3M for Boeing, the new CEO, George Buckley, needed to face the fact that the engines of new business creation at 3M had slowed. Revenues from new businesses had slipped from more than one-third to less than one-quarter. The company's reputation as an innovator dropped from number one in the Boston Consulting Group's Most Innovative Companies List to number seven in 2007. Why? The incentives of Six Sigma management gave preference to more predictable incremental innovation projects over longer-term, disruptive bets. Art Fry, a 3M veteran, noted that breakthrough businesses like Post-it Notes would have never come out of the new system. "You have to go through 5,000 to 6,000 raw ideas to find one successful business," he notes. "Six Sigma would ask, why not eliminate all that waste and just come up with the right idea the first time?"

Smart companies have found ways to fight this trend toward benign neglect and the resulting entrepreneurial atrophy. As discussed in Chapter 3, for example, Google's two founders, Larry Page and Sergey Brin, and their CEO, Eric Schmidt, meet on a weekly basis to discuss new business initiatives, thereby presenting their commitment to the ranks throughout the firm and affirming that this function remains core to what Google means as a company.

If a firm makes a commitment to fostering new business creation, these new initiatives often encounter substantially more resistance than do projects devoted to operational or business-as-usual issues. The negative reactions to such unfamiliar activities that we have observed within established firms range from simple avoidance, curiosity, and neglect all the way to active sabotage, in cases where people feel threatened by a challenge to the status quo. Clearly, senior executives must play an active part in corporate entrepreneurship in order for the new ventures to succeed. But what, specifically, should top management's role in the process be? We have identified six functions in which the senior executive team must be engaged:

Frame	Provide strategic framing
Proselytize	Validate and promote
Allocate	Allocate resources with commitment
Coach	Recruit, motivate, and educate
Track	Track performance against metrics
Embody	Lead by example

Few things are more important to guiding new business creation than an effective strategic frame, an actionable definition of the space within which a company is currently playing and intends to play in the future. There are many resources available to describe effective strategy development and framing. We won't duplicate them here; however, the salient point is to make sure that the company's stated strategy is broad enough to enable new businesses to be relevant and to take the company in directions that support its long-range objectives.

Cargill's stated strategic frame is broad, but it provides its Emerging Business Accelerator (EBA) with a context within which to select ventures that fit where the company's leadership intends to go: to be the "supplier of choice for customers in the agriculture, food and related risk management sectors." Some companies have clear statements of where they will play; some unfortunately don't. Either way, it is the corporate entrepreneur's responsibility to figure out how his or her concept fits within this larger vision and communicate it as such. Top executives must recognize that the better articulated and more insightfully designed a strategic frame they can provide, the more it will help innovators companywide to build the future the company desires.

Corporate leaders also need to proselytize on behalf of internal ventures. Use the bully pulpit by referring to innovative programs in meetings, lauding entrepreneurial successes early on to help them build momentum, and telling stories of innovative employees' efforts. Simply attending meetings focused on new business creation can send the message across the company that entrepreneurship is valued. If the company's top people don't spend time telling *and* showing commitment, then how can they expect anyone else to do so?

Allocating resources shows commitment. If you've asked a team to design and build new businesses to drive growth, make sure that team is given the appropriate resources. While some programs like IBM's Emerging Business Opportunities (EBO) have annual budgets in the tens or hundreds of millions of dollars, most are more modest, as we've seen from examples such as BP's and DuPont's Advocate Models. Either way, building new businesses requires commitment. Surging and shrinking budgets over time get in the way of productivity for any organization, but this is especially true when development horizons are measured in years. Senior leaders must not only allocate and protect resources but also recognize that, while corporate budget cycles operate in quarters and years, new business creation occurs over years or decades.

Executives who are interested in growing new businesses from within should also consider how to grow new business builders from within. While effective coaching can benefit anyone across the company, it can have a particular impact on corporate entrepreneurs. This is a role for the thick-skinned, and project leaders typically have few colleagues engaged in similar activities. Occasional redirects and pep talks from senior leaders, the kind that show that they're actively interested and are there to help, can do wonders. When EBO project leaders met with IBM's Vice Chairman John Thompson, it wasn't just for evaluation. They engaged in monthly working sessions with Thompson and the leader of the business unit into which they expected the new business to eventually move. They would explore strategy, resources, development plans—anything necessary to help the new company succeed. Thompson saw it as his role to coach the EBO leaders through adversity and to build IBM's bench of experienced corporate entrepreneurs.

Legendary innovator and executive Donald N. Frey, head of the design team at Ford Motor Company that designed the original Ford Mustang in the 1960s and later CEO of then-Fortune 500 company Bell+Howell, related that his toughest and most important job was identifying innovative thinkers who also had the skills to build new businesses. During his years as CEO, from 1971 to 1988, Frey made a habit of meeting with groups of employees from all levels at Bell+Howell. When he met someone who he felt had the potential to be an innovation leader, he'd add that person's name to a list in the top center drawer of his desk. "Innovative people ask unique, insightful questions. They say different things than other people. . . . Inside a large company, they also have to have guts to be heard." When the company had a critical challenge to face or a new business concept to explore, Frey would call on someone from that list. One of the women he recruited started at the company as a staff assistant and eventually became the leader of a new division that she helped build. "In my 17 years at Bell+Howell, I never had more than a dozen people on that list." Corporate entrepreneurial initiatives should provide the context and top-level support necessary to discover and enable more people to pursue meaningful new growth for the company.

As with any endeavor worth pursuing, it is important to know how well you're doing, which means that tracking performance should be part of the top leaders' role. Your company's top leaders should be directly involved with setting the objectives and success metrics for corporate entrepreneurial initiatives so that everyone recognizes success when they see it. After appropriate metrics have been set, at least some members of top management need to show great interest in performance against those metrics. Then create mechanisms for regular, open assessment, such as IBM's monthly meetings with the top executive in charge of the EBO program or DuPont's direct feedback from business unit and divisional leaders engaged with the Advocate team. New business building can be so all-consuming that it is important to develop performance tracking as a discipline early on.

Most important, any CEO who is serious about internal growth must lead by example, engaging new business teams, telling stories of entrepreneurial success, and lifting up the company's future leaders. Simply setting aggressive targets for more of the same will eventually plateau. If corporate entrepreneurial teams are absent from the CEO's agenda, they'll ultimately become marginalized.

To help keep corporate entrepreneurship on the agenda, many companies employ internal boards to inject senior executives into the process. The internal venture groups of some companies, such as Cisco, Cargill, and Motorola, create advisory boards for their incubating businesses. The boards provide expertise and guidance, but they also exist to build support from influential people, both inside and outside the company. Some companies also have general leadership boards for their corporate entrepreneurship programs. Baxter's innovation leadership team (ILT), modeled on a similar group at Motorola, includes six senior executives and meets on a regular basis to review progress on major new business opportunities.

There are many ways in which senior executives can help drive internal ventures. Indeed, intentionally moving any system outside its comfort zone requires leadership.

Dr. William Perry, DARPA, and the Development of the Stealth Fighter

Earlier in this chapter, we referred to William Perry's empowerment of others to tackle large-scale corporate entrepreneurship challenges. We return to that example in the context of America's Cold War with the Soviet Union.

During the late 1970s, the Cold War was a fact of life for much of the world, but especially so in Europe, where more firepower was aimed across the continent than at any other time or place in history. The Soviet Union and the Warsaw Pact enjoyed an overwhelming advantage in conventional forces, which, for a variety of reasons, the West could not overcome simply by deploying more weapons or drafting more soldiers. The United States and NATO held a small nuclear advantage, although neither strategic nor smaller tactical nuclear weapons were considered by most experts to be viable options, given their radical destructive force and the likelihood of escalation to global conflict. The West needed an alternative.

American military leadership recognized that the West's solution to this conflict would not come from having more weapons, but rather from creating radically new and innovative weapons that were "smarter" and more technologically advanced than what existed on either side at the time. The American military needed to leverage the United States's technological superiority in order to provide offsetting advantages in the Cold War arms race.

Dr. William Perry was one of the leaders who recognized this fact and acted accordingly. A future U.S. secretary of defense, Perry joined the Pentagon in 1976 as director of defense research and engineering (DDR&E) (a position that was elevated and renamed undersecretary of defense for research and engineering in 1977). One of his first orders of business was to take his team to the Defense Advanced Research Projects Agency (DARPA), an advanced technology development organization, and explore the technologies that might enable the Western powers to significantly offset the Soviet advantage.

Stealth technology had made some progress under Perry's predecessor at DDR&E, Malcolm Currie, and DARPA's director, George Heilmeier. Test flights of experimental models, funded by DARPA, clearly demonstrated that so-called stealth aircraft could attain exceptionally low radar visibility while performing within the required specifications. Perry sought the accelerated development of a real weapons system, instructing his team to "get it done in four years." Then-Secretary of Defense Harold Brown agreed to make the development of stealth aircraft "technology limited," as opposed to "funding limited," thereby freeing up all the necessary developmental resources.

Defense developments often face two common challenges: mandated changes in mission and the redirection of funding. Programs must regularly defend their budgets against other programs and respond to the preferences of members of Congress. Perry's hands-on management protected the development of stealth technology from these forces. For example, every two months Perry chaired a special executive review panel—he retained decision authority; there was no voting. He instructed the Air Force program manager to highlight problems with bureaucratic delays, which Perry would then address personally. As noted earlier in the chapter, after a few such interventions, only a limited number of bureaucratic obstructions occurred.

Perry also created a special umbrella program office that included stealth programs for ships, satellites, helicopters, and other weapons and vehicles, along with stealth countermeasures. This office supported the underlying technology base and created a mechanism through which different stealth programs could experiment with various approaches and learn from one another. The countermeasures programs helped ensure that the high level of secrecy did not result in lack of independent review and criticism.

The first stealth aircraft, the F-117A, was delivered in 1981, five years after Perry became DDR&E, and by 1990, 59 units had been deployed. In action, the F-117A performed beyond even the highest expectations: in one of the most lopsided air battles in history, the F-117A helped the United States achieve utter air superiority over Iraq in 24 hours during Operation Desert Storm, achieving a 1,000:1 advantage in combat losses. The F-117A was a radically innovative weapons system that was developed and deployed in less than eight years and gave the United States more than a decade's advantage over any adversary, which was exactly what DARPA and the top DoD leadership had envisioned when Perry proposed his dramatic and ambitious plan.

As the example of Dr. Perry's focused and powerful leadership in the development of stealth technology proves, senior management must take the lead, set the growth agenda, and work to build a culture of trust within the organization in which innovation—whether it be a new business, a new product, or a new type of weapons system—can flourish.

The lessons demonstrated by the development of the F-117A are applicable to any large organization that is attempting significant change. Corporate entrepreneurship organizations face an inherent difficulty: because they are conceiving and developing ideas that stretch the boundaries of the home organization—the vision—special leadership efforts will be required to implement proven ideas.

This view is shared by Miles D. White, chairman and CEO of Abbott Laboratories. Speaking at a Kellogg Innovation Network Dialogue in 2007, he said, "To manage an atmosphere of innovation, you have to expect it everywhere. It has to be OK to fail (and that takes work). And you have to ask for the impossible. When you demand a truly unique and difficult question, it's amazing what people devise. Asking such questions while constraining resources pushes people toward more creative solutions."

Corporate Entrepreneurship Program Leadership

While it is necessary, senior management engagement isn't sufficient. If your company has made the decision to create a focused corporate entrepreneurship team with dedicated funding (i.e., either the Advocate or the Producer Model), then you'll need talent to lead the overall corporate entrepreneurship program, as well as the projects that make up the portfolio. Depending on how ambitious your objectives are, it typically is not enough to simply rely on a set of competent managers who as assigned to the program part-time. The most successful organizations select a fairly senior and well-respected manager to take the lead full-time, like Daru Darukhanavala at BP, Andrea Hunt at Baxter, or Robert A. Cooper at DuPont. All of these people had broad-based, high-profile responsibilities at their respective companies well before they were offered the corporate entrepreneurship mandate.

Whoever takes on the role of corporate entrepreneurship leader will encounter a different, though overlapping, set of leadership requirements from those faced by senior leaders. The activities that are relevant for the program leader include

Promote	Advocate across the company and beyond
Navigate	Become the consummate politician
Recruit	Attract and retain the right mix of talent
Coach	Motivate and enable your team
Focus	Build and balance the project portfolio
Manage the process	Oversee the portfolio and processes

Many of the corporate entrepreneurial team leaders whom we interviewed over the years have related having a similar epiphany during their first year on the job. Dr. Michael Clem, formerly executive director of worldwide franchise development for Johnson & Johnson's Ethicon Endo-Surgery, the company's new business creation entity, explained, "When I started my position leading new franchise development, I thought I'd spend 75% of my time on exciting things like new business strategy, cutting edge technologies and new business creation. . . . Instead, I spend 75% of my time just communicating with people outside Franchise Development . . . other executives in the company, other people outside Ethicon Endo-Surgery."

It surprises a lot of new corporate entrepreneurship program leaders, but promoting the corporate entrepreneurship group within the company is perhaps one of their two most important roles, the other being ensuring that the group is pursuing projects that matter. Even if the team's portfolio includes some game changers that will allow the company to dominate its markets in the future, program leaders must focus on communication and relationships across the company for a few critical reasons: maintaining support for budgets, selecting projects that matter to senior leaders, and enabling the transition of new businesses from incubation to business units during the scaling phase.

Maintaining support for budgets is an issue because many other people within the company find it difficult to understand why the firm is spending money on the future outside of what the business units already do. "We're closer to the customers, so we know best. Give us the capital, not that corporate cost center," is the standard objection. The corporate entrepreneurship group leader must continuously address this and show real, quantifiable value. Fortunately, engaging with leaders across the company reinforces the team's understanding of what will matter to the company. This, in turn, enables teams to select projects that are more likely to matter to the company. Engagement and project selection are mutually reinforcing activities if you do them right. Moreover, if you're pursuing projects that matter to business unit or functional executives, it will be much easier (though rarely easy) for the new projects to make the transition out of incubation and into the mainstream company. Transition is difficult enough with support, never mind trying to pass off even a great opportunity when the people in the business unit that is required to take it on feel no sense of ownership and never asked for the opportunity. Build with the end in mind, and that end is new business opportunities that can find the resources to scale. It is much harder to do this without the right allies.

Navigating around the company—becoming the consummate politician—supports your efforts to promote. It should be an intentional, ongoing activity. After you've taken the reins, make sure you find other senior executives who have an active interest in your group—people who are not just willing to be supportive with you one-on-one, but are willing and able to stand up for the corporate entrepreneurship group when you're not there. As corporate entrepreneurship leader, you won't be at all of the meetings where decisions are made that affect your group, so the more people you have at a senior level who recognize the corporate entrepreneurship group's value and are able to make the case, the better off you'll be. In fact, corporate entrepreneurial teams should make identifying and cultivating people who have the potential to be active allies one of their first objectives.

Moreover, *never assume senior-level buy-in.* Just because the CEO or a business unit leader allocates capital and people to a corporate entrepreneurship program does not mean that he or she will maintain that support or focus. It is up to the corporate entrepreneurship team to ensure that the right people in the company continue to see the value and maintain their support. Such support has to be earned every day, especially when it is easy for people to single out your group as a "cost center." As corporate entrepreneurship teams become focused on current projects, they can lose sight of the constant advocacy that must happen on behalf of their larger efforts. Always remember that in most cases, a corporate entrepreneurship group is by definition "noncore." It is ultimately the leader's responsibility to make sure that innovation remains on the right people's lists.

To enable your navigation and promotion plans, start by creating a map of the top of your organization. Discuss your best guess regarding how each senior leader views the corporate entrepreneurship group and innovation investments more generally. Who are potential allies, detractors, and fence-sitters? Which decision makers and influencers do you need to be sure to engage? What is their leadership style (e.g., are they outspoken, or do they work behind the scenes)? Are there important people on the fence whom you might be able to bring over to the cause? Which people could stand in the way, and what can you do about them? For all the people who are important to your group's efforts to create value and survive, create a simple plan to reach out to them, better understand their perspectives, and involve them in discussions, meetings, and programs that might help tie them into the corporate entrepreneurship group's activities. Do this intentionally.

Next, create an engagement plan, execute against it, and track your progress. We helped one senior, veteran corporate entrepreneurship leader at a large global company build an engagement plan. He and his team recognized the value of the activity and began with the best intentions. Unfortunately, the group soon reverted to a nearly single-minded focus on its portfolio of new business creation projects. It is great to be focused, but new business creation projects can easily crowd out navigating and promoting the overall corporate entrepreneurship program. A few months later, the corporate entrepreneurship group leader ended up in a CEO's staff meeting where two of his colleagues on the senior staff directly questioned the corporate entrepreneurship team's raison d'être. Those same executives had been on the engagement plan, but unfortunately, they had not been engaged. Immediately following this, the group returned promoting and navigating to its list of priorities and began updating people on its progress each week.

Recruiting depends on your team's objectives. If your mandate is to develop leading new technologies, then you'll obviously require people with deep technology skills. However, this is often *not* the case. While you'll need people who are comfortable and conversant with the relevant technologies, a new business creation group's primary requirements are, well, new business–building skills. Deep technologists are often exactly the wrong people to build new businesses. Entrepreneurial skills are things like selling and promoting, networking, business strategy, resource coordination, and project management. In many cases, you can find any deep technology expertise that you need from around, or even from outside, your company. Early on, make sure you understand what skills you will need and recruit the right people.

Companies have a habit of assigning new, young, creative people to corporate entrepreneurship teams. Such people can be of great value, but don't put them in positions where they are required to motivate resources and support from around the company. Corporate entrepreneurship groups, especially when they are focused on creating truly new businesses, require respected senior staff members, people who have a range of existing relationships and credibility. It is also a good idea to consider rotating a few people from key functions or business units through your corporate entrepreneurship teams. They could be involved part-time on projects, or even join full-time for a specified period of time. If these people then rotate back to other units and functions, you'll build a cadre of supporters who directly understand the corporate entrepreneurship group's mission, tools, and constraints. Top-performing groups have even been known to cultivate and maintain a sense of alumni status for staff members who move on. The classic example was AT&T Bell Labs, which became an exclusive, nearly legendary fraternity for technologists, even if they moved on to other roles at AT&T, its successor companies, or beyond.

Fundamentally, most people either prefer optimizing the status quo, enhancing efficiency, executing to plan, and the like, or tend toward strategic thinking, inventing the future, discovering paths to growth, and so on. Stanford University professor James March referred to these differing, complementary activities in a 1991 article in *Organization Science* as "exploiting the present and exploring the future." Perhaps the most important selection criterion is to ensure that you've got a core new business creation team that thrives in the latter. People who are exceptional executors can become uncomfortable and under-perform in true corporate entrepreneurship groups because so many things are simply unknown. One former member of a corporate entrepreneurship group at a Fortune 500 company, a self-described misfit for the team, expressed a feeling of "con-stant uncertainty . . . like I never knew if we were doing the right things." To everyone's credit, she left the corporate entre-preneurship group and returned to being a significant con-tributor to one of the company's established business units. She left with an enhanced appreciation for the role of the corporate entrepreneurship team and ended up becoming a trusted ally. Not everyone is fit for creating the future, but companies need people who are good at both, exploring and exploiting, and they need to be enabled in their own ways.

Once you've selected the right team, the corporate entre-preneurship leader's primary role is to coach. Being a corpo-rate entrepreneur is tough, and the challenges can be nonobvious and difficult to anticipate. Younger team members will require mentorship, and even seasoned managers will look to the team leader to steer them through obstacles at the com-pany's highest levels. If you've recruited people who thrive in the early stages of new business creation, you can also encour-age a sense of mission. There is something motivating about creating new things. Try tying it to your larger company's stated mission. Glenn Armstrong, vice president of business innovations at Alticor Corporation, often recalls the company's vision: "'Helping people live better lives'—that's what we're about in Innovations." New corporate entrepreneurs, in par-ticular, need coaching and support. They are by definition building businesses that do not currently fit within the com-pany's established organization charts. After your group has a few new businesses in development, consider hosting monthly sessions where the corporate entrepreneurs get together and share their challenges and solutions. The corporate entrepreneurship group leader should play the role of facilitator rather than boss, providing guidance and assistance where necessary. Though external experts can help, nothing compares to receiving guidance and insight from people who are encountering similar challenges within the same company.

Focus is critical, but it's also tricky. As mentioned, corporate entrepreneurship groups can become overly focused on the projects at hand and lose track of other critical elements, such as external networking, coaching, and portfolio balancing. Focus means different things at the project level and at the group level. Individual corporate entrepreneurs should be as focused as possible on building their businesses. More specifically, they should organize their efforts around resolving the uncertainties that they've identified and testing the assumptions underlying their plans. At the group level, focus means keeping everyone pursuing activities that in the aggregate lead to a well-balanced portfolio of opportunities, as well as keeping the corporate entrepreneurship group engaged with the right people, both across the company and externally. This means creating a strategic frame and selection criteria that everyone can understand and act on. The most effective corporate entrepreneurship groups build a clear picture for themselves and others of how their activities fit within the company's overall strategy. Clarity in this regard additionally enhances the group's case across the company. It can be difficult to defend a corporate entrepreneurship program when even the group's leader is unable to cogently articulate how it fits within the company's long-term strategy.

Finally, any high-performance group has to incorporate some form of team management: coordinating functions, metrics, feedback, and the like. While the way these activities are manifested depends significantly on the context and objectives of the group, most successful corporate entrepreneurship groups that we've seen tend to have a very limited number of coordination procedures, a few simple metrics, and quick, ongoing feedback. Most activities are managed as projects, with each project defining its specific objectives, activities, and resource requirements. Project managers take care of moving things forward. Coordination occurs through regular communication between project managers. This sounds obvious, but don't assume that coordination will just happen. Projects become everyone's focus, so regular check-in meetings can be always pushed off for "more important things." Recognize that the long-term interests of the new business creation group require connecting on a regular basis; sharing challenges, insights, and opportunities; and balancing the portfolio of projects.

Such management mechanisms should be simple and focused. Corporate entrepreneurs must remain nimble, but they also need to optimize the group's scarce resources. BP's office of the CTO employs a mandatory all-team meeting every Friday morning. It doesn't matter where you are—you will be on the call if you're not attending in person. Each team member updates the group on his or her progress and critical challenges, but the team always ensures time to discuss the future opportunities, pipeline, portfolio issues, and the like. Other corporate entrepreneurship groups include status report documents as projects graduate through different phases. This can be helpful, but you should always err on the side of simplicity. If your group is applying all the documentation and reporting of a standard line business, you're probably doing things wrong. Keep things together, but keep things moving.

Metrics at BP's office of the CTO relate to a project's progress through a set of simple, overall objectives: there should be one "game changer" in progress each year, defined as an IT oppor-

tunity with at least $100 million of quantifiable, verifiable bene-
fits accruing to BP, and a set of smaller wins referred to as "technology transfers." The team knows how many potential game
changers and technology transfers it needs to have in progress
at any time to hit this objective. Tracking this is an ongoing focus
at the weekly meetings, and it has helped lead to the group's
success. If your team's role is to support innovation within
and/or transfer new businesses to business units, consider tracking "customer satisfaction" within your business unit partners.
This can be frustrating, as many people in line businesses don't
really understand what goes into building a new business; however, if your team will be evaluated on its ability to show clear
value to business units, make sure you track the value created
and the business unit partners' perspectives. The point is, create
simple metrics focused on the team's fundamental objectives
and track progress. You'll need to have the data handy when
people start questioning why you're spending resources on a
corporate entrepreneurship group.

Note that it is not a requirement that one person performs
all of these activities. Some corporate entrepreneurship programs leverage the CEO/COO team model, reinforcing one
another with complementary capabilities. BP's Darukhanavala
excels at building and motivating a high-performance team,
navigating the $250+ billion global company, and helping to
discern and evolve an effective project portfolio. His "chief of
staff," John Baumgartner, fills the role of a chief operating officer, not only managing the infrastructure and operational functions but also assisting Darukhanavala in the strategic direction
of the team. They make an ideal partnership, especially given
the group of high-level professionals that make up BP's office
of the CTO. However, no matter how your corporate entrepreneurship team is structured, all of the leadership functions
listed earlier need to be accounted for.

A Producer Produces at Baxter International

Smart companies actively develop potential corporate entrepreneurs, or at least offer those within the organization who
have company-building experience the opportunity to further
refine and leverage those capabilities. Most companies should
have dedicated new business creation programs and/or teams,
but even companies without such entities typically have some
personnel who possess these skills and interests. These people
can be either enabled to create growth opportunities on a case-
by-case basis or included as part of a larger corporate entrepreneurship initiative.

The story of Andrea Hunt and her Non-Traditional Research
and Innovation (NTRI, pronounced "entry") team at Baxter
International illustrates how corporate entrepreneurs emerge,
develop, and ultimately affect a company's bottom line. Hunt
joined Chicago area–based medical products company Baxter
International in 1988 and rose through the ranks, leading companywide change programs such as TQM and Customer Satisfaction. The breadth of the trusted relationships she built across
the company during these successful initiatives prepared her for
her eventual role as vice president of NTRI. Founded in 2000,
NTRI was charged by the CEO, Harry Kraemer, with identifying, validating, and building entirely new businesses for Baxter
that were consistent with the company's long-term vision but
were not opportunities that would typically be pursued by business units. Concurrently, Baxter initiated an innovation leadership team (ILT) made up of six top functional executives and the
presidents of each of the business units to oversee the growth
portfolio.

In 2002, Kraemer named senior Baxter R&D executive Norbert Riedel as corporate chief scientific officer (CSO). When
Riedel first joined Baxter in 1998, he was surprised at the com-

pany's lack of innovation initiative at the time. "What struck me coming to Baxter was that Baxter was a health-care company with a rather rich tradition of innovation breakthroughs, but ten years ago it seemed that R&D and innovation had no relevance to the company," he said in 2008. That would change drastically under Riedel's direction. Andrea Hunt's incubator team reported to Riedel, and Riedel, in turn, reported to Baxter's CEO, a fact that was to be significant both for Hunt's team and for the future of Baxter.

Unfortunately, in 2004, just as the incubator hit its stride, Baxter's performance tumbled and budgets were slashed, putting the incubator's future at risk. If it hadn't been for Hunt's extensive networks throughout the company and, moreover, the CEO's and CSO's commitment to the team and its mission, NTRI would have become a casualty.

After Baxter CEO Henry Kraemer left the company in 2004, Riedel remained the senior executive sponsor who kept NTRI alive. Spending was reduced to $1 million in 2004 to 2006, and the team shrank to four, and then to three, people. Hunt's core team recognized that the firm couldn't support the portfolio of projects it had built with a budget seven times larger, so it cut back to three projects, one of which was Cellular Therapies.

Cellular Therapies Emerges as a Potential Growth Platform

Cellular Therapies, which ultimately became a core growth engine for Baxter, nearly didn't survive beyond its conception. In the mid-1990s, Baxter spun out a set of what appeared to be noncore technologies into a new company, Nexell. While Nexell received FDA approval to market a device and process for purifying a patient's own adult stem cells for oncological purposes, it subsequently failed to leverage those technologies and FDA approvals into a sustainable business. By 2002, applications were only in preclinical trials in Europe, and Nexell required significant funding if it was to continue. Faced with letting its offspring fail, Baxter acquired the rights to the products and spun them back in.

While Baxter was able to return the program to a solid footing, it found few supporters and even less funding. By 2004, when Baxter was grappling with a corporate turnaround, few people in either the business units or the corporate core were interested in attempting to find a new path for these technologies, and the program was nearly canceled.

Commenting in 2008 on the Cellular Therapies program, Riedel said, "[Cellular Therapies] has now existed for probably five years and I don't even want to tell you how many times someone tried to kill it. Many times. Even though a program like that only cost us about $800,000 a year to run, people were constantly after it. If I hadn't been strong enough to protect it, it would have died."

Meanwhile, two of Hunt's NTRI staffers, Paroo Uppal and David Amrani, recognized within the technology a range of other applications beyond oncology, and particularly a potential use in cardiac therapies. The oncology business unit would have been unlikely to recognize such opportunities and even less likely to pursue them. Non-oncology applications, falling outside the unit's focus, would probably have failed to garner support.

The core device that Amrani and Uppal proposed could be offered to health-care providers at a price below cost to seed the market, as the sale of per-use cartridges and other products would drive revenue and profits—the razor-and-razor-blade model. Amrani and Uppal's analysis suggested a total potential market of over $300 million per year and validated a serious unmet need. A significant patient population experiences angina (extreme chest pain) that does not respond to existing treatments. Most doctors believe this to be caused by low blood flow to the heart. While it is not typically fatal, it can cause life-changing or even debilitating pain. The Cellular Therapies concept hypothesized the application of the patient's own stem cells to create new microvessels to the heart. Most significant, Baxter would enjoy a sustainable competitive advantage based on a significant patent portfolio that Baxter had purchased involving the underlying CD34 cells.

Baxter CSO Riedel provided the funding and authority to pursue Phase I clinical trials for the cardiac application. While such an application is always a significant commitment, sending this concept through trials presented additional complications, as Baxter was still in the midst of its 2004 downturn. Additionally, some Baxterians failed to understand the business model, while others thought that entering the cardiac market would be difficult, as it required the company to develop new channels. While these factors did increase the risk profile of the project, some senior people attributed much higher risk to the project than was probably warranted by the data. It was certainly held to higher standards during resource allocation. Such discussions of uncertainty and risk management are inherent in early-stage projects and ultimately require management judgment. Riedel and Hunt were eventually able to make their case, but they faced significant resistance in the process.

Speaking in 2008, Riedel listed a number of reasons why some people at Baxter did not want to continue pursuing new applications for Cellular Therapies, including

"We're not in cardiovascular diseases."

"Stem cell therapy is so far into the future, it shouldn't be us who pioneers it."

"Who knows how the FDA feels about this kind of stuff? It's so new."

Riedel acknowledged that these were all valid arguments, but he also managed to counter them by saying,

No, we aren't in cardiovascular but if we are going to go into a therapeutic area that is new to us, we should do it with existing technology and product know-how to manage the risk better. I know it may not be next year or the year after, but our investors are also interested in what Baxter is going to do for them five or ten years from now. And thirdly, I know the FDA has no clear pathway but at least we can talk to them, we can map it out together. The risk is completely acceptable and low.

While uncertainty was looming as a result of both change at the top and a refocus on core businesses, many at the company questioned why Cellular Therapies should continue to be funded at all. But Riedel and Hunt mustered all of their budgetary authority and political capital to take the concept through FDA Phase I.

Fortunately, their bet paid off. The trial worked. Concurrent with the trials process, Uppal and her team continued to develop the razor-and-razor-blade business model, validate the market opportunity, and define the path to market. This opportunity required special attention. Many advanced medical products are distributed and marketed to medical specialists. But companies that build a strong reputation and capabilities around one specialty do not necessarily have any credibility or access to physicians within other specialties. While the technology's role in oncology was well understood, the company had little exposure to cardiac-care providers.

Those within Baxter who questioned the wisdom of entering the cardiology market, even with a strong technology play like Cellular Therapies, had a good point—building a presence within a new medical specialty takes time and capital. This opportunity required a strategic decision at the highest level. Hunt and her team made the case that while the market would be new for Baxter, the technology was well known and proven for other applications, and the patent protection was solid. They addressed concerns by focusing on those aspects of the project that were well known, rather than focusing on what was new.

Moreover, the Cellular Therapies team spent time up front rigorously understanding the cardiology market and designing cogent business models. It validated the market opportunity, explored payers and pricing and potential adoption rates of comparable products, and assessed internal costs and requirements for Baxter to manufacture, sell, and support the product. As Uppal explained, "At Baxter, to garner funding, you need to have a complete hypothesized business model up front. . . . It's of course chock full of assumptions . . . but you continue to refine it over time."

With a clear business model and initially successful clinical trials in hand, Cellular Therapies began the internal sales process to win support for the program, which proved to be more of a challenge than the team had anticipated. While the company's heritage selling refills for dialysis equipment suggested the power of the razor-and-razor-blade business model, the NTRI team encountered skepticism regarding the model's viability. Each patient administration of the technology would require a new cartridge costing upwards of $5,000—the "razor blade" of the system. The analogous dialysis refill products retailed for around $20. While the model was the same, it had a higher price point than other Baxter disposables. This price difference caused many people to discount the viability of the model, even though it was the same razor-and-razor-blade model.

Baxter was still building its capabilities and penetration within the health-care bio products markets, where high per-use price points were more common than in Baxter's traditional markets. As a result, convincing people of the feasibility of the business model and the likelihood of market acceptance proved nearly as difficult as selling the company on the science. The team hired a statistician to evaluate similar drugs, surveyed doctors, analyzed likely reimbursement rates, and compared these to internal costs. The results were compelling and made the case with hard data.

Nonetheless, the system had failed to build significant revenues for oncological applications, which meant that Baxter subjected the cardiac application to much higher hurdles of proof for the opportunity's revenue potential. The original Nexell product had failed to achieve anywhere near revenue expectations for cancer-related indications, so some managers within Baxter were concerned about repeating the same mistake. How could this underperforming business ultimately make a meaningful contribution to Baxter's growth simply by transferring the technology to another application?

The Cellular Therapies project team persevered, created a solid plan for engaging the cardiac community, and built a solid business case, while Riedel and Hunt continued to shepherd the program. However, while the CSO's office could keep a Phase I FDA trial protected within its confines, Phase II trials posed a greater challenge. A Phase II trial required upwards of $25 million to conduct, representing more than 5 percent of the company's entire R&D for 2007.

It became imperative for Riedel and Hunt to muster support from Baxter's core business leaders. As Hunt recalled, "It was a constant, uphill sales effort to build the support we needed, but we didn't have a choice. . . . You've got to reach out to people early and often, and just continue doing so. It's not easy to take a company in a new direction, even if it looks like just the right thing to do."

Given that Cellular Therapies did not fall within the purview of any business unit, making the case for Phase II funding presented a significant challenge. Because it meant taking Baxter in new directions, the Cellular Therapies team faced much higher hurdles in receiving funding than typical projects would. Managers often have different approaches to risk calculations when they are entering new markets for their company, and the Cellular Therapies program no doubt required much more rigorous business thinking and proof points than opportunities generated from within business units.

In order to enable funding for Phase II, Riedel and Hunt negotiated the transfer of the Cellular Therapies program from NTRI to Baxter's Regenerative Medicine Division within the Bioscience business unit. In the process, the new opportunity became a new group, Cellular Therapies, and Hunt became its new vice president and leader. While NTRI continued to support the emerging unit, reporting moved from the CSO and central R&D to the Bioscience business unit president, Joy Amundson.

This transfer began the development of a new home for Cellular Therapies, but it also posed a range of new challenges. The Bioscience division needed to work with a new entity that would be prerevenue, at least until it completed the FDA's approval process, a challenge for any operating business unit. As Cellular Therapies received the funding to enter Phase II clinical trials, expectations also increased. Concurrently, Baxter was building its capabilities across biologics, and the Cellular Therapies business required reagent kits that would be scaled up and manufactured in new ways. The Cellular Therapies device, which was originally built in the 1990s, needed to be updated.

Meanwhile, the initial NTRI team (which had been transferred to Cellular Therapies) received a prestigious internal Technical Innovation Award, despite the fact that the Cellular Therapies project was not driven by new technology. The NTRI staff once again expanded to five people and a budget of around $3 million. While Hunt maintains contact with the team, its leadership has been transferred to Nancy Schmelkin.

Schmelkin's team has since expanded the portfolio and continues to incubate new business opportunities.

So what is required from leadership at the various horizons of development, to use terminology from earlier in the book? For Riedel it's quite clear:

> *At the very early stage of incubation, call it the $50,000 to $100,000 level, at a maximum it requires a buy-in of the CEO. But if the CEO says to the operating units in, for example, an executive committee meeting, "this kind of innovation-slash-incubation is worth to me an annual investment of ten million dollars and it's not for discussion, you can review it with me but I'm not going to make a change to it because you feel differently," it has already sort of legitimized the child.*

The second stage in the process, putting your team together, is more challenging, according to Riedel. The people you want to bring to your team are often looked at as the "high-potentials" whom no one wants to give up. "The task is to say, 'I'm looking for people in your units where I need the functional input and it must be this particular profile because otherwise I don't think I can be successful.'"

And the third step in the process, acquiring funding, is more difficult still. Riedel explained:

> *For example, now that we've transitioned this cell therapy program into the bio-science global business unit I can tell you every year when we go to the budget cycle and we go to prioritize the pipeline and the investments, it is a lot easier for some strange reason for the business units to put this program on the question mark list than any of their own. . . . It's sort of like something imposed on them by corporate, as opposed to my own brainchild, and therefore not treated the same way.*

Riedel has some advice for senior leaders on helping to make transitions happen. First, he recommends that a new business should not be moved out of incubation unless the new business has attained a level of maturity that will allow it to withstand absorption into the larger business.

Second, aggressively communicate your project within the wider organization. You must give your project enough of an identity to prevent the person in the office next to you from shooting it down. Maintaining an ongoing dialogue with the people you bring into your business is also important. Be sure to check in with them regularly and make sure that things are going well, so that they feel that the leader is truly concerned and involved.

Finally, the burden is on the leader to make certain that the heads of the operating units understand in a real and concrete way what the new project or innovation means to the future of the company. Riedel explains:

> *Whoever is in charge of incubators . . . has to make the incubators be tangible to the operating units. Because if I was to go and say I think we can in five or ten or twenty years implant pig organs into humans and overcome end-stage renal disease, they would probably say, "That's interesting but I really don't have any time right now to listen to it." But if I can say, "Look, I have a value proposition that I believe is aligned with our overall strategy, is aligned even with our midterm goals, benefits from either my technology or from your channels and I want your opinion, I want to get a feeling from you as to how you feel about it." If I can't do that, then I think these incubators will always be looked at as too esoteric, with overheads I would rather live without.*

It comes down to leadership. "The person in charge has to have enough business acumen and has to be credible with the operating heads to be considered someone who is grounded enough in our realities for me to believe in," Riedel says.

Radical technology-based innovation does not necessarily require radical new technology. It often requires new business design more than technology acumen. If significant aspects of a new business concept are unfamiliar to the company, a large part of the corporate entrepreneur's role will be to convince, confirm, and cajole others to support the project, or at least stay out of its way. Having the right people on board is critical. "If you have the right kind of people, who are truly of a different mindset, and you protect them from the daily grind of an operating unit, and you ask them to be curious enough and unconventional enough in how they look at the enterprise, they come up with good ideas all the time," Riedel advises.

Speaking specifically of his team at Baxter, "The team that I had . . . was so passionate and so convinced of the real purpose of this group that it was virtually impossible to discourage them enough for them to say . . . 'I'm out of here.' Whereas people from the operating units had a real desire to be pulled in and be allowed to work on an incubator for a while. It was almost like a mental rejuvenation from the daily grind."

Lessons Regarding Leadership Support for the Aspiring Corporate Entrepreneur

The Baxter example illustrates both program (NTRI) and project (Cellular Therapies) leadership. The result was a new business within an emerging growth area for Baxter. While leadership of individual projects requires talent and focus as well, many high-quality existing resources adequately address this challenge. While most books focus primarily on product or process innovation as opposed to corporate entrepreneurship, their findings are relevant for the project manager operating within a corporate entrepreneurship context. We'd recommend in particular Gina O'Connor et al., *Grabbing Lightning: Building a Capability for Breakthrough Innovation* (2008), which is focused on nurturing breakthroughs, and Scott D. Anthony et al., *The Innovator's Guide to Growth: Putting Disruptive Innovation to Work* (2008), which, as the title suggests, is focused on discovering and managing projects that are disruptive to the current business in the sense described by Clayton Christensen.

We'd add a primary objective, and a caution, for any aspiring corporate entrepreneur. The moment you receive your first corporate entrepreneurship opportunity, make sure you find a *senior-level sponsor*. Your sponsor is someone to whom you can go when you need help, someone who will provide access to company leaders and advocacy on your behalf at senior staff meetings, as well as standing up for the project when it comes time to allocate resources. There are some things it is impossible to accomplish without active contact with at least someone at the top. If you have failed to find a committed senior sponsor after a few months of leading a new business creation project, do two things:

1. Start sending out CYA memos (seriously—you'll need them later).
2. Revise your résumé, because you're probably going to need it.

The fact is, corporate entrepreneurs need active support from the top. Compelling the resources and people from around the company to move in new directions takes persistence, acumen, and authority. If your company is serious about new business creation, then your internal entrepreneurs must be represented and supported in some manner from the top.

Don't expect project leaders to do this on their own, or you're setting them up for failure.

If you're working for a company whose top leaders are not sufficiently committed to positive change, then consider moving to a new company. Life is too short to keep your head down if you truly care about creating the future. On the other hand, though the going can be tough, there are things that passionate midlevel managers can do to help tell the story and advocate on behalf of new businesses. The most important work you can do to champion a new business—or, for that matter, anything that is substantially new to your company—is to spend as much time as possible meeting with senior leaders and other relevant people around the company. Discover who might be an ally and who might stand in the way. Bring the fence-sitters to your cause if you can by determining what might be in it for each person. Be strategic and deliberate about your corporate entrepreneurship advocacy. Such alliances will come in handy down the road and in unexpected ways.

In addition to connecting with top management, recognize the value of networking with project leaders to share experiences and insights along the way. There is nothing like relying on a team of corporate entrepreneurs within the same company who can reinforce, support, and even rescue one another. Corporate entrepreneurship is tough anywhere and has many consistent characteristics across companies, although each company presents its own unique set of cultural, structural, and contextual differences. Experienced corporate entrepreneurs can become mentors who understand not only how innovation happens but also how it happens within *your* company.

The bottom line is this: at all levels—senior executives, corporate entrepreneurship program leaders, and project leaders—consider a fundamental objective to be *engagement*. Challenge your company to build truly new businesses, identify high-potential corporate entrepreneurs from within the ranks, and offer them opportunities to contribute, illustrating the power of corporate entrepreneurship to advance careers, create new growth, and beat the competition. With the right leadership, corporate entrepreneurship can become a differentiating competency in its own right.

Summary

Most meaningful endeavors require leadership. This is particularly true for the creation of new businesses within established companies. The key elements of a senior leader's role are

Frame	Provide strategic framing
Proselytize	Validate and promote
Allocate	Allocate resources with commitment
Coach	Recruit, motivate, and educate
Track	Track performance against metrics
Embody	Lead by example

The key elements of the corporate entrepreneurship group leader's role are

Promote	Advocate across the company and beyond
Navigate	Become the consummate politician
Recruit	Attract and retain the right mix of talent
Coach	Motivate and enable your team
Focus	Build and balance the project portfolio
Manage the process	Oversee management processes

CHAPTER 6

GROW FROM WITHIN; LEARN FROM EVERYWHERE

No matter who you are, most of the smartest people work for someone else.

—BILL JOY, COFOUNDER, SUN MICROSYSTEMS

It is time for a new generation of leadership, to cope with new problems and new opportunities. For there is a new world to be won.

—JOHN F. KENNEDY (1917–1963)

Looking Outside, Worldwide

All corporate entrepreneurship involves learning, building in new ways on the knowledge that makes your organization successful today. It's more than pushing someone else's product through your sales channel or being only a financial investor. (Leave these latter opportunities to venture capitalists, or at least to a corporate venture group. Even that is debatable!) Being great at corporate entrepreneurship usually requires connecting with and learning from the outside world: other companies, entrepreneurs, university researchers, inventors, government regulators—anyone who might be important to your venture. The outside world may include overseas markets, where not only customer needs but also contextual factors are quite different. Open innovation and globalization are critical factors to understand as your company pursues growth through corporate entrepreneurship. Each trend not only offers new ways to approach innovation but also intensifies the necessity to build true new business creation capabilities.

The global financial crisis that began in 2008 underscored the increasingly interconnected nature of our world. As companies become more effective at capitalizing on global resources, the more critical corporate entrepreneurship will become as a repeatable, dependable competency. As companies respond to consumer needs in countries and conditions around the world, entrepreneurial activity will bring the power of commerce to bear not only on day-to-day concerns but also on the most critical challenges facing humanity.

Open Innovation and Innovation Brokering

The mindset of many businesses has changed fundamentally in the past decade. Rather than depending exclusively on internal knowledge and resources, companies are pursuing the range and diversity of development occurring outside their walls. Many firms have adopted more collaborative business models and improved their internal capabilities to search, refine, and integrate external knowledge and opportunities. They are abandoning the infamous Not Invented Here syndrome—an affliction of some corporate cultures in which externally developed concepts tend to be eschewed—and attempting to embrace collaboration.

Henry Chesbrough, a thought leader in the field, defines open innovation as "a paradigm that assumes the firms can and should use external ideas as well as internal ideas, and internal and external paths to market. . . . Open innovation combines internal and external ideas into architectures and systems whose requirements are defined by a business model."

The precursors to open innovation arose in the pharmaceutical and biotechnology industries during the 1980s and 1990s. New pharmaceutical products take a long time to get to market. Companies in these industries experience exceptionally high levels of uncertainty, so they pursue many paths at once. Competing in this context requires a deep and wide range of scientific knowledge and specialized capabilities from manufacturing to clinical trials management. Looking outside one's firm for partners, collaborators, or even just licensing opportunities provides a natural solution. Robert Wolcott's doctoral research, completed in 2002, found that large pharmaceutical companies that are more active external collaborators perform better than their peers over the long term with respect to both total market return and relative valuations.

Beyond the pharmaceutical and biotech industries, P&G and IBM were early leaders. P&G executives have written extensively about the development and application of what they call Connect + Develop, a play on research and development that is meant to emphasize the role of connecting people, ideas, and resources as a critical factor for innovation success. IBM invests significant resources each year in externally focused innovation programs, such as its Innovation Jams and Global Innovation Outlook (GIO) programs. Each program brings thousands of external people into the IBM fold annually to explore new markets, emerging technologies, consumer trends—whatever IBM and its broader community believe might lead to opportunities. The company takes a surprisingly open approach. Any concepts or ideas generated during GIO sessions are considered open to anyone involved. The company's leaders believe that these exploratory investments benefit IBM in the form of deeper relationships with a wider range of stakeholders and generate actionable ideas, not to mention the benefits of positive publicity and goodwill.

Recall the case of BP's office of the chief technology officer (CTO) for digital and communications technology, highlighted in Chapter 3 as an example of the Advocate Model. The CTO office has generated hundreds of millions of dollars of value to the company by finding and transitioning external technologies to a range of BP's businesses worldwide. One of the great insights of the BP case is that external players are often happy to engage in experimentation largely at their own expense, as BP provides a real-world opportunity for them to implement their products and build relationships with BP's decision makers. Negotiations over intellectual property can be delicate, and there can be difficulties marshaling BP to move at a small company pace. But organizations that are devoted to overcoming these fundamental mismatches can gain a competitive advantage by serving as the proving ground for small businesses that are on the precipice of market success. Large companies can benefit by being early adopters of technology in tested and validated ways that are tailored to their needs.

Open innovation takes many forms, including open source software development, customer communities, inventor networks, and online R&D markets. The latter offer a fascinating model facilitated by the Internet. Firms such as InnoCentive, NineSigma, and yet2.com bring together clients with scientific or technical problems with scientists worldwide who might offer solutions. Such forums have accelerated the formation of connections among disparate disciplines and industries, which are so often a fountain of innovation. For example, a consumer packaged goods client of NineSigma who was seeking a fabric care technology found a surface chemistry solution from a semiconductor research organization. A medical company seeking a biosample collection system found a solution at NASA.

These nonobvious connections are not made simply by posting problems and solutions on an electronic bulletin board. Rather, clients work carefully with these intermediary companies to develop a concise statement of the technical need in a way that is general enough to protect the client's proprietary information but specific enough to allow potential solution providers to suggest answers. These intermediaries also help clients and solution providers navigate the business issues involved in negotiating and closing deals.

In their 2007 book *The Global Brain*, Rensselaer Polytechnic Institute professor Satish Nambisan and Kellogg School of Management professor Mohanbir Sawhney named a new kind of intermediary, an *innovation capitalist*, who applies venture capital concepts to early-stage intellectual property. For instance, Intellectual Ventures LLC invests in clusters of patents relevant to particular commercialization domains. It seeks out the "diamonds in the rough" among the thousands of patents in the world and then assembles a portfolio that can be sold to companies interested in commercializing them. This consolidation creates value for its clients both by identifying high-quality patents and by covering the relevant territory, which can accelerate innovation and commercialization.

In the same book, Nambisan and Sawhney defined four models of innovation based on external networks, distinguished by whether network leadership is centralized or diffused and whether the space for innovation is defined or emergent. Crossing these two dimensions yields four basic models:

- *Orchestra* (centralized leadership, defined innovation space). A diverse set of partners collaborates around a defined architecture, orchestrated by a lead firm. Example: the Boeing 787 Dreamliner project.

- *Creative Bazaar* (centralized leadership, emergent innovation space). A lead company controls the commercialization of a broad set of innovations sourced from a diverse network, facilitated by intermediaries. Example: a music label.
- *Jam Central* (diffused leadership, emergent innovation space). Innovators network in an improvisational manner without clear leadership, moving toward evolving goals. Example: a musical jam session.
- *Mod Station* (diffused leadership, defined innovation space). Innovation is implemented by a diverse, unorganized community of users and experts around an existing, defined architecture. Example: the computer gaming industry.

While there is not a one-to-one correspondence between the four open innovation models and the four models of corporate entrepreneurship, certain connections may be discerned. The dimension of centralized leadership is common between the two frameworks. Hence, the Orchestra and Creative Bazaar models of open innovation would be expected to be most compatible with the Producer and Advocate models of corporate entrepreneurship. Indeed, members of BP's CTO office, operating under an Advocate Model, explicitly consider themselves to be Orchestrators. Cisco's Emerging Technologies Group operates like a Creative Bazaar, seeking a broad set of ideas that Cisco might commercialize.

IBM's Innovation Jam and Global Innovation Outlook also operate like a Creative Bazaar, although there are elements of the Jam Central model, too, as implied by the name. In this case, however, IBM is acting more like an Enabler and an Opportunist than like a Producer or an Advocate, as there is no specific IBM organization designated as the one that will pick up on promising concepts. Innovation Jam and GIO are not formally associated with IBM's Producer effort, Emerging Business Opportunities (EBO), although ideas that have come out of them have been adopted by that program. For example, Joel Makower of GreenBiz reported that the 2006 Innovation Jam generated opportunities in green technology. Some of this translated into an EBO known as Big Green Innovations in 2007.

These cases are excellent examples of how open innovation, pursued as a general innovation strategy, can work together with a formal corporate entrepreneurship effort. Ultimately, firms that are capable of leveraging multiple approaches build powerful innovation competencies as well as more options for successful growth.

Globalization and Corporate Entrepreneurship

While corporations explore the power and pitfalls of more open approaches to innovation, globalization generates an environment of intensifying competition, diversifying markets, and proliferation of consumers worldwide. There is perhaps no dynamic greater than globalization compelling companies to master new business creation. Back in 1998, a Louis Harris & Associates survey of 308 CEOs found that "globalization" was judged to be the most important trend affecting companies. The trend has only accelerated since that time.

While some firms, such as Royal Dutch Shell and IBM, have been global in character and strategy for decades, for the most part the concept of a "global economy" has emerged as a common factor in corporate boardrooms only since the turn of the century. The demands of serving diverse customers in varied conditions was complex enough when most of the world's formal economic activity occurred in selected parts of the Pacific Rim, Europe, and North America. The relatively recent rise of major economies all over the world, from South America and South Asia to Africa and the Middle East, has intensified the challenge. Companies that are eager to serve these fast-growing markets must consider a much wider range of needs and factors. What works in Tulsa or Tokyo might not work in Tashkent.

For most of corporate history, entering emerging markets often meant opening a sales and service office and providing essentially the same products to the local market that the company would provide in its home country, typically the United States, Europe, or Japan. While many companies consider themselves "global"' simply by virtue of having a presence in many countries, a truly global company appreciates the differences among consumers and contexts in the varied markets it serves. Selling the same products in the same way around the world does not make a company global. Engaging with markets on their own terms and serving the unique needs of customers in varied locations worldwide while maintaining the competencies and culture that make a company great— these are the characteristics that distinguish truly global firms.

As a result of accelerating globalization, many of the best long-term growth opportunities have been shifting to developing economies. While there are similarities, the realities of doing business differ among countries and regions, sometimes dramatically. While this is not a book about globalization per se, globalization compels companies to recognize that playing in varied markets requires an ability to design businesses that are suited to different conditions. The complexity is clear, but if competing in varied contexts were easy, then there would be no money in it. The profit opportunities will accrue to those who figure out how to serve consumers with business systems suited to the local environment. Factors such as infrastructure, supplier base, differing regulatory regimes, and, most important, varied consumer preferences often require new business design and creation capabilities. Companies that master local specialization while retaining the benefits of global breadth will prosper.

Selling shampoo in New Delhi that was developed for consumers in Cincinnati is no longer good enough. One of the highest-margin products in P&G's portfolio is a small sachet of shampoo sold in India. Many lower-income consumers in India, typically women, consider shampooing a luxury, something that they would do more often were it not for the cost. The large bottles sold in developed countries not only are too expensive but are difficult to distribute across India's complicated infrastructure and to manage within the channel of the small retail kiosks that are common throughout the country. Large bottles take up too much space and are too expensive for most consumers. Thus, P&G created small packets of shampoo, known as sachets, which provide consumers with an occasional luxury. Though they sell at a much lower price, the margin per ounce turns out to be much higher than that of similar shampoo sold in developed countries.

But achieving growth in diverse markets means much more than simply redesigning products. It requires new approaches to the business design. P&G's sachet solution helped manage the supply chain and retail channel issues, enhanced the customer experience (i.e., prior to this, many consumers had not had access to high-quality shampoo), and changed the way P&G captured value. Think about this in terms of the Innovation Radar described in Chapter 2. It illustrates how any company can approach the entry into a new market in terms of holistic new business design.

In some cases, the demands of launching new businesses in emerging markets generate new business models that would have been unlikely in developed economies. Take the emerging phenomenon of microfranchising. Microfranchising is similar to microfinance, where individuals and institutions provide small loans (often in the $25 to $500 range) to enable independent entrepreneurs to become self-employed. The practice was pioneered by Grameen Bank in Bangladesh in the 1980s. Microfinance organizations have since proliferated within developing markets worldwide. Microfranchising combines the scale of microfinance with the developed-world concept of franchising. Instead of requiring tens or even hundreds of thousands of dollars to launch a franchise, microfranchising provides very poor people with the know-how, products, and support materials necessary to initiate and grow a business.

Microfranchising helps address the lack of jobs and skills necessary to start new businesses, the lack of products available for very low income communities, and the insufficient understanding and interest of most companies regarding serving and operating in these communities. Drishtee of India provides an example. Founded in 2000, this for-profit company provides a common information and communications technology infrastructure for use by village franchisees who own the local node. This allows the franchisee to provide not only Internet access to Web-based services such as online health and education but also a range of products and services as diverse as Internet access, cell phones, insurance, and even reading glasses. The entrepreneur charges the villagers modest fees, then returns a percentage to Drishtee. Researchers P. Clint Rogers, Jason Fairbourne, and Robert Wolcott reported in a 2009 working paper for the Brigham Young University Center for Economic Self-Reliance:

The Drishtee model has already made an impact. . . . By 2008, Drishtee had successfully demonstrated this concept in about

2000 kiosks in 12 states across India, with plans to keep adding thousands more. Each Kiosk caters to approximately 1200 households, a majority of which have an aggregated income of less than $2 a day. Over a longer period, Drishtee is geared up to try to become a type of "electronic Wal-Mart," so to speak, for the rural world.

While Drishtee did not arise from within an established corporation, it clearly illustrates a nonobvious new business design that is capable of operating profitably in exceptionally challenging environments. As emerging enterprises like Drishtee begin to prove the microfranchising model, it is likely that larger companies will eventually define their own approaches to these markets, just as some have begun doing with microfinance.

While fundamental human needs may be consistent, the numerous ways in which they are manifested within varied geographies, cultures, and economic environments ensure that the quest for global growth will compel more and more companies to adopt the tools and practices of corporate entrepreneurship. Operating in world markets is no longer simply a challenge of overseas sourcing and selling; instead, it requires competing against companies with increasing sophistication and customization on behalf of local markets. Corporate entrepreneurs, armed with the tools of new business design and development, provide a potent force in this context.

Corporate Entrepreneurship in Times of Trouble and Plenty

Historically, corporate entrepreneurship efforts have been cyclical. To some extent, such efforts follow the ebbs and flows of the broader economy or conditions in the industry sector. Many large companies undertook corporate entrepreneurship initiatives in the 1960s, only to cancel them during the downturn of the 1970s. When business is good, increased profits make internal funding easier, and some of that gets invested in corporate entrepreneurship. When business is bad, firms often slash long-term investments as part of larger cost-cutting measures.

Robert A. Burgelman and Liisa Välikangas, in their 2005 MIT *Sloan Management Review* article, suggest that the cycles of corporate entrepreneurship activity are more complex than that, varying with corporate strategy and context. Indeed, when times are good, firms may have ample opportunities to grow just by exploiting their core. Without the impetus of a major challenge to the core business, as happens during lean times, the desire to invest in the future can wane. One of our clients put it well: "How do you argue with success?"

In many cases, though, corporate entrepreneurship efforts are shuttered because they don't produce the expected results quickly enough. Management underestimates the time and effort required to see a major impact. Moreover, many early programs tended to be overly focused on technology, as described in Chapter 1. Sometimes companies select the wrong kind of management, people who may be exceptional at what they do but are unsuited to the task of business building. All of these situations reflect a lack of clarity concerning the objectives of the program. Some programs overextend themselves, for example, falling into the culture change trap discussed in Chapter 1. Burgelman and Välikangas put it well: "The rise and fall of corporate venturing, incubators, and other innovative new business development programs since the 1970s may have been due in large part to lack of clarity as to the role and limits of entrepreneurship and innovation in new business system development within large corporations."

So, what is one to do? As we've emphasized throughout this book, think carefully about your long-term strategy before initiating a corporate entrepreneurship program, and then "keep it sold" through ongoing networking and communication. In good times and bad, always make sure that your team achieves, documents, and communicates smaller, quantifiable wins as well as the triumphs. You can't be assured that home runs will occur soon enough or often enough to maintain senior management's dedication. Make sure your portfolio can always answer the question, "What have you done for me lately?" In hard times, it will be especially important that you keep even the board of directors involved and aligned with the long-term promise.

Kellogg School of Management professor Andrew Razeghi recently outlined in a 2008 working paper ("Innovating through Recession: When the Going Gets Tough, the Tough Get Creative") some of the advantageous opportunities that arise during a downturn. The unmet needs of the market are easier to discern during a period when customers are thinking harder about their spending. Engagement with the market in new and creative ways is possible. Downturns also provide an opportunity to deepen your relationships with existing customers. Staying in front of customers keeps your brand relevant in their lives. This is particularly true if you use the opportunity to deliver new kinds of value. (Conversely, cutting prices or reducing advertising and other communications can backfire, compromising customers' perception of the value of your brand.)[1] Finally, as many observers have noted, recessions provide an opportunity for strong and brave companies to grab market share. In a 2002 study of 1,000 companies from 1982 to 1999, McKinsey & Company researchers Richard F. Dobbs, Toman Karakolev, and Francis Malige found that those that invested in strategic acquisitions and new opportunities (consistent with corporate strategy) during the recession of 1990–1991 retained or gained market leadership.

One of our colleagues in the Kellogg Innovation Network, a former Fortune 500 CEO, shared a technique for influencing decision makers at her prior employer to motivate and maintain investment in critical projects: start a rumor that the competition is doing it!

Along the same lines, venture capitalists and competitors may be waiting for you to let your best ideas and people go. Vinod Khosla, a founder of Sun Microsystems and one of the world's top venture capitalists, described the business environment from his perspective in a March 2009 *Wall Street Journal* article:

> MR. MURRAY: *What about general economic conditions? Credit availability, the ability to launch any of these investments as IPOs. How does that affect your calculations?*
>
> MR. KHOSLA: *I'm sort of a permanent optimist. I actually think this is a great opportunity. Yes, we can't do an IPO. But I'll tell you every advanced project at Dow is being shut down, or at DuPont or at your favorite technology company. Those are the people who have the creative ideas, who will do the most advanced stuff, so the number of opportunities we are seeing with start-ups is going up.*

It is inevitable that some corporate entrepreneurship programs will be scaled back or canceled. Those are times when corporate entrepreneurs and leaders may be forced to fly below the radar, undertaking more pilot programs and learning efforts than full-fledged new business development. It is always a good idea to identify the critical uncertainties in a corporate entrepreneurship project and attempt to undertake brief, inexpensive experiments to resolve them. During a downturn, it may be necessary to do so to maintain at least some progress.

To the Future

The global financial crisis that began in 2008 underscored the increasingly interconnected nature of our world. While some leaders and their citizenry might long for a more insulated or even isolated existence, the reality is that we rise or fall together. While the primary objective of corporate entrepreneurship at the company level is to provide a potent path to sustainable, meaningful growth, the macro implications are enormous.

As independent entrepreneurs continue to drive the "creative destruction" described by Schumpeter in the early twentieth century, globalizing corporations are increasingly joining the race. And it is not a zero-sum game. Open innovation practices are marrying the capabilities and resources of large enterprises with the ingenuity, passion, and vision of researchers, inventors, and entrepreneurs, both inside and outside corporations.

As companies respond to consumer needs in countries and conditions around the world, entrepreneurial activity will bring the power of commerce to bear not only on day-to-day concerns but also on the most critical challenges facing humanity. The power of the market, sometimes nudged and cajoled by government, focuses entrepreneurial energy on market needs that might result in value for investors. There are few more compelling opportunities for value creation than providing economically and environmentally sound energy for global growth or eradicating disease and poverty. Nobel Peace Prize winner Muhammad Yunus's call for a new commitment to what he calls "social business"—for-profit enterprises sustained by workable business models, but whose primary mission is social in nature—suggests yet another avenue for corporate entrepreneurs to make an impact in the world. Large corporations have a great deal to gain, even beyond the goodwill and positive press associated with social action. As illustrated by the Danone-Grameen partnership described in Chapter 1, business can "do well by doing good." In the meantime, companies like Danone are learning powerful lessons about serving vast swaths of the human population, knowledge that will serve these companies well as global markets expand and consumer requirements diversify and evolve.

Rather than running counter to the pursuit of profit, these epochal challenges present organizations of all sizes with some of the most compelling opportunities for profitable growth. The entrepreneurs, innovators, and managers who engage these issues might also find themselves rewarded with a deep sense of meaning that is often missing from business as usual. For the right people, there are few things more gratifying than nurturing a concept from idea to marketplace success, especially when that idea is accompanied by a mission of consequence. Jerry Porras, Stewart Emery, and Mark Thompson put it well in their 2007 book, *Success Built to Last*: "Healthy, sustainable societies require the creation of healthy, sustainable organizations, and great organizations and societies can only be built by human beings who can grow and create meaningful success."

Entrepreneurs generate much of the growth and many of the new jobs in market economies. Entrepreneurship enables people to envision and create the future, something that is perhaps the fundamental path to a prosperous world. Despite inherent challenges, large global corporations have all of the ingredients to excel at the endeavor and the scale to make a significant impact, and many are upping their game. It is everyone's responsibility—business, government, academia, and nonprofits—to create the context in which people can discover and manifest innovative solutions for human needs and desires. As the world's population nears nine or ten billion in the present century, the only way to build the kind of world we hope our children and grandchildren can live in will be through a fundamentally sound, vibrant entrepreneurial sector. The good news is that we can all play a part.

The more rapidly environments change, the more adroit organizations must become. As we've seen, companies as diverse as DuPont, Nokia, Cargill, and IBM have transformed themselves multiple times in their more than 100-year histories, while most companies rarely survive past a decade. An environment that is supportive of corporate entrepreneurs can help companies assemble a portfolio of options on future outcomes, providing multiple paths to the future and enabling more rapid transformation. If even a small number of leading corporations learn the art of new business creation, their competitors must eventually respond or fade.

As globalization intensifies and competition diversifies, and as companies become more effective at capitalizing on external concepts and technologies, corporate entrepreneurship will become more critical as a repeatable, dependable competency. Companies that master new business creation build a bulwark against obsolescence, generate vital paths to growth, and offer top talent compelling opportunities to create the future.

Note

1. Razeghi reports on an organization that decided to skip a trade show in order to cut costs. As a result, customers wondered if the firm's business was in trouble and began seeking alternative suppliers.

INNOVATION RADAR CONCEPT DEVELOPMENT QUESTIONS

What (Brand, Offerings, Platforms)

1. Could this concept include proprietary platforms and standards that could sustain our competitive advantage?
2. What does "upgrade" or "improvement over time" mean for this concept? What are possible upgrade paths?
3. What are some possibilities for modularity and common designs or architectures? Will our design permit upgrades to be installed more quickly and cheaply than comparable offerings?
4. What common and/or off-the-shelf technologies or processes might we exploit?
5. What opportunities exist to integrate outside technologies and/or capabilities into our products and services?

Who (Solutions, Customers, Customer Experience)

6. In what ways can we segment our target customers to enhance the appeal, marketability, and/or market size of this concept (psychographics, demographics, application, geography, size/volume, function, and so on)?
7. Specific appeal: For each of the customer segments that our concept might target, how can we modify the concept to better serve that segment?
8. Broad appeal: Alternatively, how can we define the concept to appeal to the broadest market possible? Can we target new customers for the company as a result of this concept?
9. How can this concept lead to better solutions for specific industries, vertical markets, or customer segments?
10. How might we augment this concept with complementary services?
11. How can this concept be expanded to create integrated, end-to-end solutions for our customers?
12. How might we combine products and services from outside vendors?
13. What customization possibilities can we include to permit this concept to be tailored to the requirements of individual customers?
14. How does the buying process for this concept differ from that of competitive offerings?
15. How does this concept affect the way we interact with customers in any context (e.g., buying, delivery, support, or service)?
16. In what ways might we incorporate interacting with, observing, and/or engaging directly with customers as a result of our concept?

17. How can we build feedback and customer knowledge mechanisms into our concept?

How (Value Capture, Processes, Organization)

18. How might new pricing schemes (e.g., subscription pricing, "pay-as-you-go," or value-based pricing) help us to
    - Make our offering more accessible/attractive/ convenient for our customers?
    - Improve our working capital requirements (e.g., accelerate payment)?
    - Share risk with suppliers, customers, consumers, and/or other partners?
19. How might pricing discrimination differentiate among different customer segments?
20. What types of licensing opportunities could be involved in this concept that might provide revenues for our company? (This question can relate to the modularity and customization questions in the "What" section.)
21. How might frequency and loyalty marketing programs play a role in this concept?
22. What role might intellectual property play?
23. Does this concept offer opportunities to enhance internal business processes to reach higher levels of operational effectiveness or efficiency, in this or other parts of our business?
24. What role might information technology play in automating and/or reengineering our business processes to support this concept? (For example, how might innovative learning and/or knowledge management processes enhance this concept?)

25. Will this concept benefit from unique hiring, personnel development, or incentive programs for employees, partners, external experts, or others?
26. How might partnerships and alliances with external organizations enable and/or enhance this concept's success?

Where (Supply Chain, Presence, Networking)

27. How might our company's supply chain be affected by this concept?
28. What challenges and/or opportunities are important to consider regarding this concept? For instance:
    - New ways of sourcing inputs and delivering our offerings to market
    - Opportunities to remove supply chain layers and reduce costs
    - New ways of planning and forecasting demand
    - New ways to interact with our supply chain partners, including IT and Web-based technologies
    - Opportunities and/or challenges in outbound logistics and shipping
29. What types of alternative channels might we consider to best deliver our products and services to our customers and/or consumers? (Examples include direct and indirect channels, online, brick-and-mortar, big-box retail, small independent retail, wholesalers, dealer networks, and so on.)
30. For this concept, should we consider changing the way we manage our existing channels? For instance,
    - Can various channels be integrated in ways that better serve our customers?

- How might we better serve specific customer segments through customized channels?
- How might self-service play a role in our channel strategy for this concept?

31. How might networking technologies enhance this concept by
    - Enhancing the functional value to the customer/consumer?
    - Enabling data collection on product and/or service performance?
    - Recording customer usage and/or other behavior?
    - Employing, upgrading, and/or servicing our products and/or services?
    - Enabling more effective interaction with our customers?

HISTORY OF CORPORATE ENTREPRENEURSHIP

Labs Rule!

With the coming of the Industrial Revolution, wealth and power came to be based on manufacturing. By the mid-1800s, political economists noted that industrial productivity increasingly depended on the application of science and technology to industry. German economist Friedrich List wrote in 1841 in his book, *The National System of Political Economy*:

> *There scarcely exists a manufacturing business which has no relation to physics, mechanics, chemistry, mathematics or to the art of design, etc. No progress, no new discoveries and inventions can be made in these sciences by which a hundred industries and processes could not be improved or altered. In the manufacturing State, therefore, sciences and arts must necessarily become popular.*

In the decades that followed, Germany introduced an organizational innovation: the corporate research and development (R&D) laboratory. Companies such as Hoechst, Bayer, and BASF were early adopters. Other companies in Europe and the United States followed their lead. Around the beginning of the twentieth century, large U.S. companies, beginning with those in chemicals and electronics and then spreading to most large manufacturing industries, set up centralized R&D labs to drive innovation. General Electric, AT&T, DuPont, Corning, and Kodak led the way. According to Richard Rosenbloom and William Spencer in *Engines of Innovation*, between 1919 and 1936, U.S. manufacturing companies established 1,150 industrial research laboratories. The number of industrial research professionals (scientists and research engineers) employed by these companies grew from 2,775 in 1921 to 27,777 by 1940.

World War II fostered the "Age of Big Science." Companies such as General Motors, General Electric, Westinghouse, AT&T, and IBM, in partnership with government laboratories and universities, supported the war effort with both industrial production and technological capabilities. The atomic bombs dropped on Hiroshima and Nagasaki made the whole world aware of the awesome power of large-scale applied science and technology. On August 6, 1945, sixteen hours after the atomic attack on Hiroshima, President Harry S. Truman made a public statement: "We have now won the battle of the laboratories. . . . What has been done is the greatest achievement of organized science in history."

Vannevar Bush, director of the U.S. Office of Scientific Research and Development during World War II, captured the mood of the time in his 1945 report, *Science: The Endless Frontier*. The report promoted what came to be known as the "linear model" of development, the idea that investment in high-quality science would provide a foundation for new technologies that could be turned into a cornucopia of profitable products. Additional companies opened or expanded their corporate labs. Government facilities that had originally been conceived as temporary were transformed into national labs. The National Science Foundation came into being, which, along with the Office of Naval Research, became the major government supporter of basic research in the United States. Frederick Terman, one of Vannevar Bush's students at MIT, fostered academic-industrial partnerships with companies near Stanford University. With the help of early U.S. government funding—by 1960, the U.S. Department of Defense was funding 70 percent of electronics R&D in the country—those partnerships begot today's Silicon Valley.

Leveraging discoveries from their R&D labs, companies looked to their operating divisions to conceive and build innovative products. This model was generally productive in regulated industries, such as military hardware and pharmaceuticals, and in heavily science-based industries, such as advanced materials and electronics. But by the 1970s, many companies began questioning the value of their investment in R&D. Their labs did not seem to be generating commercially useful results often enough, and few blockbuster products could be traced back to the labs. Companies of all types were struggling with commercializing new technologies, particularly those that could not find ready application in existing product divisions. Possessing the best science was insufficient. Companies needed better ways to create viable opportunities based on what they were learning in their labs, and better ways to realize economic value.

Separate or Imitate?

In response to the problem of commercialization, some companies created separate organizations dedicated to finding and developing opportunities that did not fit, or even conflicted, with existing divisions or were too long-term for organizations with short-term P&L responsibilities. Lockheed's "Skunk Works" was a pioneer, founded just before World War II. It turned out a series of high-profile successes, including the U2 and SR-71 spy planes and the F-117A stealth fighter. In 1966, Hewlett-Packard consolidated its long-term science and emerging technologies research in HP Labs, which drove the company's move into computer and information technologies. Many of the technologies developed in HP Labs were translated into products that came to account for most of the company's revenues and growth for years. A few years later, in 1970, Xerox Corporation founded the Palo Alto Research Center (PARC) for much the same purpose.

Sometimes a company would set up a separate team to pursue specific new concepts. In 1980, IBM sent a dozen engineers to Boca Raton, Florida, to design and build what it dubbed the "personal computer," or PC. Freed from IBM corporate policies and cultural assumptions, the group devised an innovative architecture and business model for the PC. By 1985, according to John DeMott's report in *Time*, there were ten thousand employees working in what became the IBM Entry Systems Division. Similarly, GM launched the Saturn Corporation in 1987 as a completely separate company. Automobile manufacturers would routinely set up subsidiaries to pursue new concepts, but these subsidiaries might share corporate design, engineering, manufacturing, or back-end capabilities. Saturn was completely independent and introduced several changes in design, production, and marketing that would have been nearly impossible to do within GM.

The nature of the connection between the separate group and the parent corporation depended on the perceived sources of conflict with existing business units that motivated the separation in the first place. Hans Brechbühl of the Tuck School of Business noted in 2006 that typical problems for new business concepts include different performance metrics, different cost structures, and cannibalization of existing products, which presents problems when the new concept is sold through existing sales forces. The IBM PC group, for instance, broke a sacrosanct IBM tradition by selling through retailers rather than exclusively through IBM's vaunted sales organization. Saturn eschewed GM's product development processes and, most visibly to the public, its dealership sales practices.

To this day, a great deal of research suggests that using a separate organization is typically the most effective way for a large company to develop innovations and bring them to market in situations where the capabilities necessary for the innovation to succeed are significantly different from the company's capabilities, its dominant processes, or its core values. When a designated group is assigned this task on an ongoing basis, however, the separation can make it difficult for the company to recognize and exploit the opportunities. Xerox's failure to capitalize on numerous revolutionary innovations from its Palo Alto Research Center is one of the most poignant examples. PARC invented or incubated laser printing, Ethernet, the modern personal computer graphical user interface of windows and icons, and the modern computer text editor, among many other things. Other companies, most famously 3Com and Apple Computer, garnered the lion's share of profit from successfully commercializing these inventions. But Xerox was certainly not the only company to underestimate the value of emerging computation technologies. Hewlett-Packard lost the first-mover advantage in this space as well. Steven Wozniak presented his idea for a microcomputer to his Hewlett-Packard bosses in 1975, but they declined to do anything with it, so he left and started Apple with Steven Jobs.

Over time, many companies came to the conclusion that their corporate laboratories and separated new business groups were not sufficiently successful in developing opportunities that their business units could or would pursue. Dedicated, protected new business development teams often operated more like enhanced, privileged versions of centralized R&D than like truly alternative corporate entrepreneurial groups. In the extreme, conglomerate pioneer Harold Geneen of ITT wrote in 1984 in his book *Managing* that "entrepreneurism [sic] is the very antithesis of large corporations." Some companies spun out their corporate labs as independent contract research companies that would continue to do business with the original parent company but could also pursue other opportunities if sufficient internal interest could not be generated.

Rather than set up a separate new business development organization, other companies tried to reinvigorate their internal conceptualization and commercialization prowess by emulating the practices and culture of an acknowledged leader. For instance, 3M was famous in the 1960s, 1970s, and 1980s for consistently introducing new businesses built around innovative technology platforms. A look inside the 3M organization revealed two particular factors that accounted for its ability to repeatedly generate new businesses: 3M allowed its engineers and scientists to (1) spend up to 15 percent of their time on projects of their own design, and (2) seek resources and mentoring from anywhere in the company, should an individual's immediate supervisors reject requests for support. Joe Bailey, a VP of R&D in 1999, noted in 3M's 2002 self-published history, *A Century of Innovation*, that "the most successful people at 3M were good at getting out of their offices, meeting people, interacting and knowing where to find the expertise they needed." Teams could form flexibly around new business concepts, and, if these concepts were successful, the individuals involved might take up leadership positions with a new 3M division dedicated to the new business. Starting in 1984, teams could also find support from a corporate grant program to fund research that had not yet qualified for budget support through ordinary channels. In the 1990s, the company selected strategic program areas and provided additional corporate-level funding.

Attempts by other companies to implement 3M's practices often failed, as entrenched incentives and processes thwarted such flexibility. It usually was not possible to transplant the innovative practices and culture of 3M to other corporate contexts. Commenting on 3M's practice of giving employees 15 percent of their time to work on projects of personal interest, Dr. Nelson Levy, a former vice president of R&D and president of various global pharmaceutical companies, quipped at a Kellogg Innovation Network meeting in 2004, "I might as well give my people 15 percent paid leave!"

In your company, can you imagine people doing end runs around their bosses? How risky would that be for their careers? Gifford Pinchot, in a 1987 article in *Research Management*, provides a compelling example of how the culture and leadership at Hewlett-Packard allowed for this. David Packard bestowed an Award for Meritorious Defiance, "For contempt and defiance above and beyond the call of engineering duty," upon a Hewlett-Packard researcher in 1982. That researcher, Charles House, in response to Packard's demand that a project be terminated—Packard instructed, "When I come back to this laboratory next year, I don't want to see this product in the lab"—had instead adopted an alternative interpretation and, with the tacit approval of his local management, moved the product into manufacturing and successful sales within the year! Can you imagine this happening at your company?

Note that we do not recommend that companies attempt to adopt the practices of the historical 3M or HP unless they have a strong history of organic innovation and new business development. Even then, it's risky. Willful defiance of senior management is more likely to be a quick trip to a pink slip than a path to growth. It is difficult to see how this could be a manageable, sustainable approach for most companies.

Toward Global, Services-Oriented New Business Development

By the mid-1980s, the linear model of innovation was no longer widely accepted. Indeed, in the United States and Europe, the simmering concerns of the 1970s had turned into a full-blown crisis of confidence, beginning with heavy industry and moving to high-tech over the decade, as first Japan and then other Asian economies captured increasing market share. The success of Japanese quality control and production management and enhanced overseas competition led companies to scale back or spin out their central R&D laboratories. In their stead, greater emphasis came to be placed on rapid, incremental, production-oriented innovation, a capability that was perceived to be a factor in the rise of Japanese manufacturing companies.

Another important aspect of Japanese product improvement methods was the integration of customer needs early in the design process, often by actively engaging customers in innovation efforts. Eric von Hippel's *The Sources of Innovation* in 1988 showed how, in many cases, such understanding of customers could be more important to project success than discovering and developing new technologies. Large companies began implementing formal processes for cross-disciplinary and cross-functional teams to bring together the technology, production, and marketing capabilities necessary to bring a steady stream of relevant and valuable product improvements to market.

Concurrently, new metrics and methods for monitoring innovation projects and programs were devised, particularly for the early stages of the innovation process: the so-called fuzzy front end. Companies instituted formal practices for generating, collecting, and evaluating new ideas. Phase-gate (also known as stage-gate) methods became popular, as researchers and practitioners recognized that innovation could be rationally managed with deadlines and deliverables, performance tracking, and standardized procedures across projects. Effective implementation of phase-gate processes enhanced innovation performance through more efficient allocation of resources, smarter early-stage development, and greater management visibility into progress. Not that there weren't problems. Heavy-handed implementation of such processes, with metrics that are inappropriate for early-stage concepts, can prematurely kill promising new opportunities. For instance, it is often not possible to define the return on investment of an early-stage concept. Inflexible stage-gate processes don't work well for truly new concepts, but well-adapted stage-gate applications can add significant value. It takes companies some time to develop the capability at various horizons.

As U.S. and European firms implemented and adapted the quality control and product improvement methods pioneered by Japanese companies, they began to look for new ways to achieve competitive advantage, beyond incremental innovation. Unaided, few people are naturally good at thinking beyond what already exists. Substantial, game-changing innovation often arises from discovering needs that customers don't even know they have until they are fulfilled. To develop more substantial new business concepts, leading companies have become more deliberate and sophisticated about uncovering customer needs. Examples include empathic design, ethnographic research, and customer activity cycle mapping. But to make such deep investigations worthwhile, companies have had to revisit what they do with the insights generated, i.e., how to move these insights into development and generate substantial new business opportunities without relying solely on the technology-focused centralized lab structures of the past.

Part of the answer was R&D partnerships. Michael Porter's research in the 1980s revealed the importance of innovation networks, particularly geographical clusters of specialized companies and institutions that collectively generated better-than-average productivity gains. In industries that were deemed to be nationally strategic, such as semiconductors and aerospace, the U.S. government facilitated and subsidized the pooling of R&D in formal R&D consortia that previously would have faced antitrust barriers. Soon after the turn of the century, the economic growth of countries such as China, India, and Brazil encouraged companies to open local R&D facilities to serve these markets and interact more directly with other local companies in the industry ecosystem. New forms of international R&D partnerships emerged, fostered by advances in and diffusion of information and communication technologies.

Corporate venture capital offered another potential solution. When large corporations scaled back or abandoned their laboratories, burgeoning private venture capital partially filled the gap. Venture capital financing for new business development soared in the 1990s, not infrequently for ventures conceived by stymied employees who were leaving large corporations. Partially in an effort to recapture some of the benefits of their entrepreneurial employees, large corporations began setting up their own venture funds. Rather than exclusively attempting to generate technologies in captive laboratories, some companies sought to access technologies that had been developed externally, often before they reached the market. In profitable but fast-moving markets such as electronics and semiconductors, where resources were available, technology changed rapidly, and competition was fierce, many corporate venture groups thrived. Two of the pioneers, Intel Capital and Motorola Ventures, returned billions of dollars of value to the parent company. Robert A. Burgelman and Liisa Välikangas reported in a 2005 issue of *MIT Sloan Management Review* how, at many companies, corporate venturing efforts tended to be scaled back when fortunes changed. Moreover, they were often vulnerable to changes in leadership and strategic priorities.

The Internet boom of the late 1990s further encouraged large, established companies to rethink both threats to their core businesses and new market opportunities. A few began and sustained new approaches to seeking growth from within. Some of the earliest efforts at deliberate new business creation began in 1999 at companies such as DuPont, IBM, and Whirlpool and continued with entrants throughout the 2000s, such as Cargill, Cisco, and Motorola. Also, the increasing role of services relative to manufacturing in modern economies broadened the focus of corporate innovation efforts beyond technologies and products. Industrial companies like DuPont and GE derived more and more of their revenues and margins from knowledge and services, often wrapped around core products like chemicals or aircraft engines. By 2005, only a minority of DuPont's revenues came from selling bulk chemicals. Even technology stalwarts like IBM and HP built massive services businesses. By 2008, over half of IBM's business focused on services. Companies as diverse as McDonald's, Target, and Bank of America formed innovation teams dedicated to conceiving and prototyping new kinds of consumer experiences aimed at growth and customer satisfaction.

Taken together, companies in the late 1990s began experimenting with new ways to drive organic growth through regular, repeatable new business development. Today, these efforts span industry and geographic boundaries. Many of them seek to realize value across the full spectrum of what companies do and how they add value in the marketplace.

FURTHER READING

Managing Innovation

Anthony, Scott D., et al., *The Innovator's Guide to Growth: Putting Disruptive Innovation to Work* (Boston: Harvard Business Press, 2008).

Burgelman, Robert A., and Liisa Välikangas, "Managing Internal Corporate Venture Cycles," *MIT Sloan Management Review* 46(4), Summer 2005, pp. 26–34.

Christensen, Clayton M., and Michael E. Raynor, *The Innovator's Solution: Creating and Sustaining Successful Growth* (Boston: Harvard Business School Press, 2003).

Drucker, Peter F., *Innovation and Entrepreneurship* (New York: Harper & Row, 1985).

Garvin, David A., and Lynne C. Levesque, "Meeting the Challenge of Corporate Entrepreneurship," *Harvard Business Review* 84(10), October 2006.

Hargadon, Andrew, *How Breakthroughs Happen: The Surprising Truth about How Companies Innovate* (Boston: Harvard Business School Press, 2003).

IBM Global Business Services, "Expanding the Innovation Horizon," Global CEO Study, 2006.

Johnson, Mark W., *Seizing the White Space: Growth and Renewal Through Business Model Innovation* (Boston: Harvard Business Press, 2010).

Leifer, Richard, et al., *Radical Innovation: How Mature Companies Can Outsmart Upstarts* (Boston: Harvard Business School Press, 2000).

Markides, Constantinos C., and Paul A. Geroski, *Fast Second: How Smart Companies Bypass Radical Innovation to Enter and Dominate New Markets* (San Francisco: Jossey-Bass, 2004).

McKinsey Global Survey on Innovation, "How Companies Approach Innovation," 2007.

O'Connor, Gina, et al., *Grabbing Lightning: Building a Capability for Breakthrough Innovation* (San Francisco: Jossey-Bass, 2008).

Wolcott, Robert C., and Michael J. Lippitz, "Innovation Management in Large Corporations," in Hossein Bidgoli, ed., *Handbook of Technology Management* (Hoboken, N.J.: John Wiley & Sons, in press).

Developing Innovative Concepts

Belliveau, Paul, Abbey Griffen, and Stephen Sorermeyer, eds. *PDMA Toolbook for New Product Development* (New York: John Wiley & Sons, 2002).

Burns, Andrew, and Stephen Evans, "Empathic Design: A New Approach for Understanding & Delighting Customers," *International Journal of New Product Development and Innovation Management* 3(4), 2002.

Charitou, D., and C. Markides, "Responses to Disruptive Strategic Innovation," *MIT Sloan Management* Review, Winter 2003.

Chesbrough, Henry, *Open Business Models* (Boston: Harvard Business School Press, 2006).

Day, George S., "Creating a Superior Customer-Relating Capability," *MIT Sloan Management Review* 44(3), Spring 2003, pp. 77–82.

Nalebuff, B., and I. Ayers, *Why Not?: How to Use Everyday Ingenuity to Solve Problems Big and Small* (Boston: Harvard Business School Press, 2006).

Nambisan, Satish, and Mohanbir Sawhney, *The Global Brain: Your Roadmap for Innovating Faster and Smarter in a Networked World* (Upper Saddle River, N.J.: Wharton School Publishing, 2007), p. 123.

Stewart, Alex, *The Ethnographer's Method* (Thousand Oaks, Calif.: Sage Publications, 1998). For an update, see *International Journal of Market Research* 49(6) (Ethnography Special Issue).

Thomke, Stephen, "Enlightened Experimentation: The New Imperative for Innovation," *Harvard Business Review*, February 2001.

Vandermerwe, Sandra, "How Increasing Value to Customers Improves Business Results," *MIT Sloan Management Review* 42(1), Fall 2000, pp. 27–37.

Innovation Frameworks

Adner, Ron, and Daniel A. Levinthal, "The Emergence of Emerging Technologies," *California Management Review* 45(1), Fall 2002.

Baghai, Mehrdad, Stephen Coley, and David White, *The Alchemy of Growth* (Reading, Mass.: Perseus Press, 1999).

McGrath, Rita Gunther, and Ian MacMillan, *The Entrepreneurial Mindset* (Boston: Harvard Business School Press, 2000).

Porter, Michael, *Competitive Advantage* (New York: Free Press, Macmillan, 1985).

Von Hippel, Eric, *The Sources of Innovation* (New York: Oxford University Press, 1988).

Innovation History

3M, *A Century of Innovation* (St. Paul, Minn.: 3M Corporation, 2002).

Baumol, William, *The Free Market Innovation Machine: Analyzing the Growth Miracle of Capitalism* (Princeton, N.J.: Princeton University Press, 2002).

Bush, Vannevar, "Science: The Endless Frontier," Report to the President, July 1945 (Washington, D.C.: U.S. Government Printing Office, 1945).

Rosenbloom, Richard, and William Spencer, eds., *Engines of Innovation* (Boston: Harvard Business School Press, 1996), Chapter 1, "Evolution of US Industrial R&D," pp. 13–85.

Schumpeter, J. A., *The Theory of Economic Development* (Cambridge, Mass.: Harvard University Press, 1934).

Smith, Douglas K., and Robert C. Alexander, *Fumbling the Future: How Xerox Invented then Ignored the First Personal Computer* (New York: William Morrow & Co, 1988).

Van Atta, Richard, et al., "Science and Technology in Development Environments," paper P-3764, Institute for Defense Analyses, Alexandria, Va., March 2003.

INDEX